"Rubietta beautifully presents Jesus's gentle yet persistent summons to... experience abundant comfort when life hurts, relief is scarce and help is absent or inadequate.... Poignant stories illustrate each chapter's take-away;...Rubietta richly [presents] Jesus's beckonings with dynamic story-telling, emotionally inviting prayers, and calls to honest introspection. She is wonderful at expressing the heart's longing for comfort and care. Evangelicals will find their spirits uplifted after relishing [this] entreaty to draw nearer still to the Jesus who always cares."
—*PUBLISHER'S WEEKLY* STARRED REVIEW

"Eloquent words. Powerful imagery. To borrow Jane's own words, *Come Closer* 'rocked me from my roots and set me in motion' toward an even more intimate relationship with the Lover of my soul. Jane speaks to the heart of every woman who longs for a genuine encounter with Jesus."
—SHANNON ETHRIDGE, best-selling author of *Completely His*

"An invitation to come from wherever you are right now to an intimacy with Christ that is deeper, higher, wider, and more personal than you've ever experienced. Jane skillfully woos the reader to develop the daily habit of responding to His call. If you are longing for a transformational encounter with Him, read this book!"
—CAROL KENT, speaker and author of *A New Kind of Normal*

"Jane beckons us to accept Jesus's invitation to join Him in intimacy. My response is immediate and core: I'm on my way!"
—ELISA MORGAN, CEO OF MOPS INTERNATIONAL,
publisher of *Fulfill*

"I love this book! Jane Rubietta's powerful words bring Scripture to life and shine its dazzling light into our lives. She paints such a vivid portrait of Jesus that His loving invitation 'come unto Me' is tangible on every page. More than any other book, *Come Closer* showed me Christ's heart and drew me into the warmth of His loving embrace."

—LYNN AUSTIN, Christy Award-winning author of
A Woman's Place

"Inspiring and practical, Jane's insights on Jesus's words bring the encouragement we need to RSVP to Christ's ongoing opportunities for a life with no regrets."

—BECKY HUNTER, president, Global Pastors' Wives Network,
and author of *Being Good to Your Husband on Purpose*

"Jane helps move every reader into the life-transforming shadow of the loving Savior. *Come Closer* is a breath of fresh air for the soul."

—PAM FARREL, author of *Woman of Influence*

"Has there ever been a cultural time when invitations to intimacy have been more desired? *Come Closer* will make you want to consider those points of deepest connections—in your own soul, with God, and with others."

—KAREN MAINS, director of Hungry Souls and author of
Open Heart, Open Home

"Jane invites the reader to exit the highway of life and find refreshment in God's truth. She gently leads you to the feet of Jesus answering His invitation to 'come.' Because of her, I know myself better and my Savior more intimately. Don't miss this invitation to experience life to the fullest!"

—JILL SAVAGE, executive director of Hearts at Home and
author of *My Heart's at Home*

15 Invitations from Jesus to...

come
closer

A Call to Life, Love,
&
Breakfast on the Beach

Jane
Rubietta

WATERBROOK
PRESS

Come Closer
Published by WaterBrook Press
12265 Oracle Boulevard, Suite 200
Colorado Springs, Colorado 80921
A division of Random House Inc.

ISBN 978-1-4000-7351-1

Published in association with the literary agency of Alive Communications Inc., 7680 Goddard Street, Suite 200, Colorado Springs, CO 80920, www.alivecommunications.com.

Library of Congress Cataloging-in-Publication Data
Rubietta, Jane.
    Fifteen invitations from Jesus to come closer : a call to life, love, and breakfast on the beach / Jane Rubietta. — 1st ed.
        p. cm.
    Includes bibliographical references.
    ISBN 978-1-4000-7351-1
    1. Spirituality. 2. Spiritual life—Christianity. 3. Jesus Christ. I. Title.
    BV4501.3.R83 2007
    248.4—dc22

                            2007010096

Printed in the United States of America
2007—First Edition

10 9 8 7 6 5 4 3 2 1

• • • • •

To my husband, Rich,
Who taught me to love Christ the Word
And the Words of Christ,
Always with "Come Closer" welcoming laughter and love.

And to Bill and Amy Chapin,
Who kept coming
Into our lives with the light.

The Invitations of Jesus

The "Come" Passages in Scripture

John 10:10   "I came that they may have life, and have it abundantly."

John 11:43   "Lazarus, come forth."

Mark 10:21   "Looking at him, Jesus felt a love for him and said to him, 'One thing you lack:… come, follow Me.'"

John 1:38–39   "Rabbi…where are You staying?" He said to them, "Come, and you will see."

Matthew 8:7   "I will come and heal him."

Matthew 11:28   "Come to Me, all who are weary and heavy-laden, and I will give you rest."

Luke 19:10   "For the Son of Man has come to seek and to save that which was lost."

John 14:18	"I will not leave you as orphans; I will come to you."
John 15:26	"When the Helper comes...the Spirit of truth..."
Mark 10:14	"Permit the children to come to Me; do not hinder them; for the kingdom of God belongs to such as these."
Luke 11:33 (NIV)	"No one lights a lamp and puts it in a place where it will be hidden, or under a bowl. Instead he puts it on its stand, so that those who come in may see the light."
John 7:37	"If any man is thirsty, let him come to Me and drink!"
John 21:12–13	"Jesus said to them, 'Come and have breakfast.'... Jesus...took the bread and gave it to them, and the fish likewise."
John 14:3	"I will come again and receive you to Myself, that where I am, there you may be also."
Revelation 22:12, 20 (NKJV)	"And behold, I am coming quickly." "Amen....come, Lord Jesus!"

Contents

PART 3:

breakfast
Food & Care for the Soul

PART 4:

homecoming
Heaven

Acknowledgments

Where would I have landed without a broad net of protectors and catchers around me, people who have loved me and held me and challenged me to come closer to Jesus so I could come closer to who he created me to be?

Bouquets of gratitude and thank you, thank you to:

Jack and Shirley Henderson and Jim and Marie Rubietta, my parents by birth and by marriage. You have been powerful influencers for good in my life.

Phil and Lois Whisenhunt, a.k.a. "Mom and Dad Whiz," and their daughter, Beth, who adopted me into their family when I was a skinny college intern in a strange country.

Lynn Austin, Joy Bocanegra, and Cleo Lampos, my writers' group, who keep challenging me to come closer to excellence as both a writer and a woman who seeks God.

Adele Calhoun, Karen Mains, Linda Richarson, Marilyn Stewart, and Sibyl Towner, mighty women who hold fast to me, that "Christ might be formed" in me.

Shirley Mitchell, whose laughter and love always renew my heart.

Marge Rockenbach, who has prayed for me through yet another year.

Ruthie, Zak, and Josh, our children, whose honesty and love have kept me on the rails.

Rich, whose love and grace humble me daily.

And, in the words of Zechariah, father of John the Baptizer,

"Praise be to the Lord, the God of Israel, because he has come and has redeemed his people" (Luke 1:68).

Accepting the Invitation

The boy's feet barely reached the edge of the airplane seat; the tail on his seat belt after buckling stretched farther than his legs. He nibbled his lip, brow furrowed, concentrating on the coloring book his mother provided. I peeked over my seat, smiling at his small blond head.

A flight attendant's voice issued warnings about tray tables and life preservers. The plane nudged almost imperceptibly away from the ramp and toward the tarmac.

Just before sticking in earplugs for takeoff, I heard a cherub voice ask, "Almost there, Mom? Almost there?" A slight pause as he peered out the window. "Almost there?"

Even as I grinned—we weren't even to the runway yet, let alone "there"—my heart twisted. His innocent query echoed some deep but ignored longing. Oh, to be almost there.

Throughout life we ask, whether whining from a car seat just after leaving or elbowing a sibling or gripping the armrest with terror, "How much longer? Are we almost there?" We grow up with the plaintive words on the tip of our tongue.

We are always traveling, always en route, always wondering if this is our stop. But where is "there"? On the commute to work, "there" is the job. At the other end of the shift, "there" is home or family, or a sofa to cradle a work-weary body, or a Crockpot simmering a welcome, or a letter from someone we love. Perhaps "there" is college, or the first apartment, or the shelter of marriage, or the security of a job. Society tells us that "there" is the Hollywood body or the massive paycheck or the new house or the next rung on the ladder. "There" always seems one step removed from where we currently are.

Beneath the question "Are we almost there?" and its easy answer of "No!" hides a haunting sense that "there" is just beyond our reach. Home isn't quite it, family not exactly the spot, the job definitely a hollow substitute. Yet the question clings like our shadow. The longing lodges in our hearts—like too much rice swallowed too quickly. A faint rumble of dissatisfaction, thought that this is not the right piece for the jigsaw puzzle, not close enough to ease the tension of the search and the underlying hope.

So we press on in this pressurized world, searching, perhaps, for perfection. The perfect job, or spouse, or home, or child. The perfect parents or the perfect past or surely a perfect future.

Instead, we have broken relationships, broken tools, broken promises, broken childhoods. Brokenness reminds us that this is not heaven, but heaven's coming.

come along with me

Come Closer actually began for me as I contemplated the enormous hospitality of God—it mystified and fascinated me how he loves and graces such a stubborn and sinful bunch of people like me. I was sick of my own sicknesses, all leering and ugly. The breadth of God's hospitality overwhelmed me. I couldn't grasp or even frame such a vast subject, until I realized that God's hospitality is ultimately and powerfully shown in Christ's coming to us.

The letters of Matthew, Mark, Luke, and John—people who lived with Jesus, followed him around, and responded to his offer, "Let's do life!"—record conversations rich with invitation. I reread them, stopping at the many references where Christ invited the people to "come." I was captivated and so excited that I started smiling, love-struck because of who this Savior turns out to be.

This eye-opening look at Jesus and his invitations became this book—and it's an invitation to you to look at Jesus like you never have before.

come closer

You'll notice Jesus is very practical. He gets right to the point. He asks hard questions. This book is designed to provide a spiritual adventure, whether you're reading it on your own or as a group, ministry, church, or Sunday school. The chapters are structured to apply to your life, right where you are, so we can discover together this welcoming Jesus, interact with him through the Scriptures, and allow him to invite us into changed living—to change our hearts because our lives intersect with the Savior.

"Come," he says, over and over.

The elements of each chapter create a type of liturgy for us, a dance between us and Christ, a structure into which God may be pleased to speak to us, a predictable place where our own hearts and needs can meet the heart of Christ. Here you can take notes on your soul, reactions, and God's whispers to your heart. A separate journal might also be a good place to record your journey as you hear and heed Jesus's invitations. Each chapter begins with the words of Christ. Try reading them out loud, even though there may be only four words. Sit with that sentence, letting his words roll through your mind and then into your heart. (You'll find the list of his key invitations in the front of this book.)

Next is a stanza from a hymn. If you know the tune, sing! If not, use the words as an entry point for God to begin speaking, and prep your mind and soul to receive what follows.

As you read the chapters, make the text your own. Underline, highlight, question, journal, disagree, or pray through the words. Throughout each chapter, ask this of Jesus: "Come. Make yourself clear to me. Speak to me. Change me." This is a prayer Christ loves to answer.

At the end of every chapter are even more direct invitations. Here are some other thoughts on how to get the most out of these sections.

come and consider

Imagine what Jesus might say to you today, or what you might whimper or weep to him, if you were sitting next to him on the sofa or walking along a dusty country road together like the disciples were privileged to do. This is an interactive time with Christ. Maybe you'll want to read this section out loud and gauge the reaction of your soul. Use this to meditate, being still and listening to the life and hope the Lord offers.

come for life

This is what God has said in Scripture. Read this section slowly. Ask God to show you how it applies to your life, how it fits with the chapter's invitation from Christ, and how he wants to use those words to encourage and love you or challenge you to a deeper place.

come closer

These questions invite us to talk about where we've journeyed with Jesus during our reading. In a lonely world, there are few people who love us enough to ask us gentle but probing questions about our lives, hopes, sorrows, pain, and sin. These are questions you might ask me, or I might ask you, if we were to work through these subjects over a cup of coffee or tea and a handful of dark chocolates. Keep track of your answers in your notebook or journal, so you can record what God is doing in your life.

come home

This prayer will help take you through your fear, past pain, and present struggles, and into Christ's presence. This is a relinquishment place where you can lay down heavy burdens and be swept away by the Lover of your soul.

come today

This is a challenge to recap the invitation and make shifts in your life. Just as folks in real estate talk about the importance of "location, location, location," those of us seeking to plant Jesus in our hearts understand "application, application, application." After all, what difference does the gospel make if it doesn't make a difference, right? So this is where you can ask God to sweep you off your feet, to disarm you, and change you.

• • • • •

We are not meant to white-knuckle our way through this earthly journey, hoping for heaven someday. In Jesus's words and invitations, find the promise of life now. Abundant, healing, joyful life.

On the plane, when the little boy lifted his chin and asked, with eyes full of hope, "Almost there?" I heard a different answer. I didn't hear his mother say, "No, not yet; not for a long time."

I heard Jesus say, "Come."

PART 1
· · · · ·

life
Abundance

come
for abundance

"I came that they may have life,
and have it abundantly."
—John 10:10

· · · · ·

I'll trust Thy love, believe Thy word,
    Lord, I'm coming home....
    My strength renew, my hope restore,
    Lord, I'm coming home.

WILLIAM KIRKPATRICK

He is fourteen. Tall, lean, full of exuberant, exhausting life. As I perch at our family room window, wondering blankly about the most life-giving thing I could do, he races up our hill, turns some cartwheels, cups his hand to his mouth, and erupts with a shofar sound. And keeps running.

At 6 feet 1½ inches tall and 145 pounds, our son runs, laughs, jiggles, fidgets, talks, shouts, and plays the piano like he lives his life: fortissimo and fast.

He is less worried about accuracy on the notes than he is about zest and gusto.

He makes mistakes. He runs into things, breaks the occasional dish, bumps into chairs and doorjambs because his long limbs make big wide movements.

He has lows, but they are infrequent and brief. The buoy doesn't stay under for long before bobbing to the surface. He spreads joy indiscriminately, like dandelion seeds in a breeze.

I think Jesus must love this puppy-dog boy very, very much, because he is so like Jesus.

He is, in fact, Jesus's namesake. Joshua. *Yehoshua.* God is my salvation; the God who saves. And in Joshua, I see lived out before me daily Jesus's words in John 10:10: "I came that they may have life, and have it abundantly."

He is fourteen.

I am not.

And he is my new mentor.

Longing for Life

Doesn't everyone long for more life, for life like that? For a sense of fullness and vitality and goodness to exude from their heart, through their pores, and out into their relationships in the world? Weakly, I can state that I'd like to be more alive. It seems like a nice idea. I'd like to feel alive, energetic, and fully engaged with the person or task before me.

Perhaps this is a personality issue. Maybe outgoing people, or cholerics (or whatever those tests label them), thrive on being with others and have this zest, and everyone else is left wading in the low energy, nonabundant gene pool. Or maybe the abundant life was a limited edition offer, a time-sensitive possibility, and we didn't return our envelope in time.

Surely Christ's promises are not limited by personality tests or time.

Even so, LIFE in capital letters no longer seems to come naturally to many of us—not such exuberant life, not boisterous, engaging, laughing life.

We drag ourselves out of bed in the morning, make lists, slog through the day, do our work. And energy? Maybe after enough coffee or chocolate (or both in my case), but the high evaporates quickly, replaced by irritability. Eye contact—what's with that? We avoid people's eyes so that they don't expect something from us that we cannot give. And laughter? Ha! When holding a microphone, I seem to be funny. But daily? Not so much. I often don't even notice things are funny until the time for communal laughter has long passed. When I'm most alive, I laugh easily. Unfortunately, I'm not laughing much these days.

We're not exactly dead women walking. But we're definitely dazed, half-alive.

Costly Contentment

I don't think this is the picture Jesus painted when he said, "I came that they may have life, and have it abundantly." But, hey, we make it through our days, fulfill our commitments, smile when appropriate. Isn't that enough?

Maybe I'm just planting seeds of discontent in women's hearts when talking about longing for more of life. After all, the apostle Paul said he had learned to get along in all kinds of situations. And if he can say that about his life, which was full of beatings and poisonous snakes and being dropped over walls and shipwrecked, well, we need to just put up or shut up.

Don't we?

I mean, some would suggest that simply watching out my family room window trying to think of something zany to do was wrong. I wasn't being content with the life I already had. Somehow, contentment seems to slant us as passive passengers in the canoe, paddles on our laps. We exist in an emotional neutral and let the current carry us.

Frankly, that's a lie. Although it fits with the paralyzed image many have of Christianity, the lack of longing is a problem.

One friend, my mentor for years, e-mailed me this a few months ago: "What sounds like fun to you? I'm thinking about us spending the better part of a day together. Design a perfectly happy day, and let's try and launch it."

Guess what? I couldn't come up with anything that seemed right. What if she laughed or yawned at my idea? Or it fell flat like old soda pop? Why couldn't I think of something crazy—happy—to do?

Something is seriously wrong when we don't long for life. We have so deeply buried our longings that we can't access them anymore, like longings are some archaic computer language that no longer relates to current equipment.

But beneath our performance, perfectionism, and brokenness lies a common longing, if we excavate enough layers. Occasionally, as we sigh and wipe our brow or our tears, there exists, just beyond the known, just at the edges of our being, a hope for another world—a thought that there must be more: like a three-dimensional pop-up book instead of this black-and-white printout.

So why do we pursue hope's fulfillment in the wrong places, expecting heaven on earth in relationships, jobs, husbands, children, careers, or house and home?

One woman's answer made me laugh. She grinned wryly and divulged her latest hobby: triathlons. "It's the bored housewife syndrome," she explained. "It's this or have an affair."

There are options other than having an affair (and exercise)! Too many of us try this: work harder, smile more, do more, run faster. And when that doesn't work, we pretend.

Meanwhile, the chasm between our promised abundant life and our day-to-day existence widens. And this is where we're left: we're torn between disappointment *(Is this it? Is this all there is?)* and hope *(Are we almost there?).*

Do You Wish to Get Well?

Jesus's primary purpose was to reverse the curse—life is his *raison d'être*, his reason for coming! The gospel of John alone records the word *life* nearly fifty times.

Jesus talks about life frequently—to the Jewish authorities, the lame, the lost, the bewildered, the heavy-hitting sinner. He offers life whenever it is opportune, especially on the Sabbath.

In John 5, Jesus comes upon a man who has been sick for thirty-eight years. Day after day, the man plops down at the pool, hoping an angel will materialize and ruffle the waters, hoping someone will hustle past, stop, drop him into the pool first, hoping for healing. Jesus halts with a soul-piercing question, a dive-to-the-bottom-of-the-problem question: "Do you wish to get well?" (verse 6).

In other words, what do you long for? What do you really want, sitting here day after day?

The man avoids answering, describing instead his waiting process. After medicating with self-pity, he hears Jesus: "Get up, pick up your pallet and walk" (John 5:8). Immediately the man is healed. He stands, rolls up his mat, and launches into his 3-D life on new limbs.

The Jewish authorities catch him carrying his pallet on the Sabbath and pounce, more interested in the Law than in the life represented by the bundle he carries. Do they recognize him as the man who always huddled in a heap by the sheep gate? Are they looking for evidence of healing, for signs of life?

No. And frankly, too often, neither am I.

Like the authorities, who want to snare the healed man with the letter of the Law, pointing fingers and assigning penalties, I watch for people who color outside the lines and I fumble for my whistle, ready to blow. I don't notice the healing, the progress, the creativity, the life in another, as much as where they fall short.

Jesus's offer of life on the Sabbath—imagine that!—so offends the leaders that they begin persecuting him (verse 16). In the rest of John 5, Jesus offers testimonies proving that he came from God. In verses 39–40, he says, "You search the Scriptures because you think that in them you have eternal life; it is these that testify about Me; and you are unwilling to come to Me so that you may have life."

Life. And they were unwilling to come. They were busy about legalities and technicalities and making sure everyone else was in perfect compliance. They wrangled about distances and weights and pointed to the Law of Moses to justify their obsessive behavior.

This hurts my heart. How often do I resist Christ's invitation, refusing to relinquish pain and problems, unwilling to come to him?

Unwilling to Come

Sometimes the honest answer to Jesus's question, "Do you wish to get well?" is, "Not really. Not so much; not too badly." As long as we aren't well, we have an excuse. We don't have to participate fully in the course presented to us or the options available; we make allowances, not expecting as much of ourselves but expecting more of others. Not being well provides us with unhealthy opportunities for self-indulgence, mollycoddling, and grasping for attention. Maybe the unwellness is anger, bitterness, unforgiveness, anxiety over relationships, or some other means of keeping people at arm's length.

Sin makes us unwilling to come to the Author of life. When I relish the brick and mortar I stack between myself and another, hoping my distance and isolation strategy will garner attention and sorrow on another's part, I sin. And part of me dies. Because any time I move away from relationships, I move toward death. And away from Jesus.

Jesus said, "For whoever wishes to save his life will lose it" (Matthew 16:25). My resistance of relationships, my walls of separation, my legalism, and my whistle-blowing are all lifesaving techniques. I don't want to get hurt, so I hypercontrol everyone and everything around me. I'm so preoccupied trying to protect myself that I don't head for home.

To really live, we have to be willing to give up our life, to stop trying to save ourselves embarrassment, risk, pain, and problems, and give it up to the Author of life. We must release our tenacious grip and control efforts and throw ourselves into Christ's arms, wholeheartedly accepting his offer. Life, abundantly.

The Thief Comes...

We move toward home, toward those deep but hidden longings, when we move toward Christ. But beware. Jesus prefaces his offer of an abundant life in John 10:10 with a startling statement that I am prone to ignore: "The thief comes only to steal and kill and destroy; I came that they may have life, and have it abundantly." An intruder creeps into the house, bent on destroying the very life Jesus offers. This is not petty theft—some cat burglar sneaking around for our silver candlestick or a loaf of bread. This is outright murder. This enemy will lie, connive, depress and suppress us, snuffing out life's sparks at every opportunity. He will try to twist our longings, convert them to something shameful, and use them to lead us into death, deception, decay, and sin. We know that drill, have danced those steps for too many years.

And too often, the Enemy has a conspirator in crime. We collude with this thief, cooperating with the subterfuge, refusing Jesus's offer of life. What steals our joy? What robs us of passion?

Abundant possessions become stones around our neck. "Be on your guard against every form of greed; for not even when one has an abundance does his life consist of his possessions" (Luke 12:15). My husband was dismayed when we left the house and the doorknob came with us—Fixer-up Chore No. 163 on his evergreen list. He joins Thoreau, who was convinced that our belongings detract from the quality of life rather than add to it. We love our home, thank God for our abode, but truly, possessions should not be confused with abundance. Hefting the load of ownership bows our back. We are dragged under the waves by the anchor of duty, the weight of obligation, the bulk of financial responsibility. The waters of work bury us, when all the while, Jesus invites us to live weightlessly—to walk on water!—by holding his hand.

Relational crises, when reinforced by the Enemy, can be twisted into an opportunity to abandon commitments. We ditch relationships because they don't feel life-giving. "Bag the marriage if it doesn't get you where you want to be," the Adversary encourages. "Leave your family. Drop your best friend. Run away." But are our relationships stealing our life? Or is it not breathing deeply of Christ's life in the midst of them that robs us of abundance?

Past pain is an accomplice in the holdup. Relationships inevitably bring pain—pain that is difficult to surrender. A woman I know, Marta, can cite from memory a long list of people's sins against her, dating from childhood all the way up to yesterday morning. Are they legitimate grievances? Absolutely. No one should have to endure such ugliness growing up. Is holding on to the pain helping Marta heal? No. Her death grip on past injustices drains the cup of life offered to her and poisons the cup of life she is to extend to others.

Unforgiveness plunders our daily lives and past pain fouls present living. The Thief lies to us, telling us that the other person deserves nothing from us, that we have every right to withhold forgiveness. And so we nurse our hurt until it curdles into resentment and bitterness.

Past sin can also collaborate in crime. In Psalm 51:3, David cries, "For I know my transgressions, and my sin is ever before me." He mourns his adultery with Bathsheba, his desperation to get his own way, his murder of her husband. Whenever the beautiful Bathsheba appeared, the reminder of his sin haunted David.

My sin haunts me when I see my children, my husband, my neighbor—when I feel my faults as a nurturer, when I'm aware of my not-enoughnesses. I don't:

pray enough
be still enough
worship enough
give enough
serve enough
love enough
act enough
forgive enough
go deep enough
feel enough
laugh enough
live enough
I am not enough.

But here's the good news: Jesus is enough. He's more than enough. And we can't hear it enough—his words: "I came that [you might] have life." Life! "Vitality" in the original language. Not just something that will be good in heaven after we die, but vitality now. Not in dribs and drabs or Depression-era rations. No, life abundantly. Literally: "I came that you might have life, superabundantly, beyond measure." A lot of life, a blue whale lot of life.

And yet here we are, clutching the dock and slipping around in the shallows, on the rocks, with a minnow net.

Paul uses the same word for abundantly in Ephesians 3:20, "Now to Him who is able to do exceedingly abundantly above all that we ask or think, according to the power that works in us" (NKJV). It is totally unrelated to anything we can be, seize, or achieve. It is entirely related to Christ's power, Christ's life, working within us.

Contrast that overwhelming, exceeding abundance with the thieving, killing, destroying Intruder. Haven't we experienced enough death?

Death of innocence

Death of a childhood

Death of a dream

Death of a relationship

Death of hope

"The thief comes" versus "I came." My heart leaps in response to Jesus's words. I want to grab my pallet and grasp that life, run after it, hold on to it, be transformed by it.

When we respond to Jesus's offer of life this way, when our heart quickens and we begin to run for his arms, we are almost there. We embrace 1 Timothy 6:12, "Fight the good fight of faith; take hold of the eternal life to which you were called." Heaven will be great—one day. No more tears, no more death, no more pain. When the roll is called up yonder, we'll be there, and we can laugh—then.

But Jesus offers us life now, today, when he says, "I came," and holds out his hands.

When our children just toddled about, thick-legged and eager to explore everything, they would hold up their hands to their daddy, so tall above them. Rich would reach down, grip their empty, open hands in his, and spin around—the child an extension of his arms. The children flew out like the paratrooper ride at the amusement park, laughter pealing as their daddy's large hands engulfed their small hands.

They didn't even need to hold on, because his iron fist wrapped around them.

So today, I hold out my empty, open hands to Jesus and wait for him to wrap his nail-scarred ones around me. As he picks up my heart and spins me about, my laughter mingles with my tears, and I whisper through a trembling smile, "I'm here. I come."

• come and consider •

When Jesus says, "Come,"
he is saying, "Follow me.
Follow me to the desert.
Dance with me at the wedding.
Feed the five thousand with me.
Enter into my joy.
Sit at my knee.
Laugh at my analogies.
Overturn the tables.
I lug the child, heal the lame, raise the dead.
Enter into my life.
Come.

To do so means you are willing to die—
to your fears,
to your hope for safety in this world,
to your preoccupation with your possessions, your
        public image and your private self.
Follow me to the cross,
and to the life that never ends,
but begins, now.
Come.

Laugh with me, weep with me,
sit with me, watch with me,
walk with me, live with me.
Follow me.
Come."

• come for life •

For I have been crucified with Christ; and it is no longer I who live, but Christ lives in me; and the life which I now live in the flesh I live by faith in the Son of God, who loved me, and delivered Himself up for me.

Galatians 2:20 (NASB, 1977)

• come closer •

- Make a list of your longings. How are they buried or paralyzed?
- What do you clutch in your hands that prohibits your coming for life?
- Where is the Thief operating?
- How do possessions, pain, and sin keep you from abundance?
- Imagine Jesus holding out his arms, reaching for you. How do you respond?

• come home •

Oh God,
No longer will I allow the Thief
to steal my life from me.
I wish to be well!

To pick up the pallet of my life
and run for your arms.
I release my fears, my past,
my lost dreams and not-enoughnesses
and receive your life.
Abundantly.
In Jesus's name,
amen.

• come today •

How will you come today for life?

come
from death

"Lazarus, come forth."
—John 11:43

· · · · ·

Come, my Way, my Truth, my Life;
    Such a Way as gives us breath:
    Such a Truth as ends all strife:
    Such a Life as killeth death.
        GEORGE HERBERT

A t 1:00 in the morning, I finish preparing most of the first round of food. I set the alarm for 4:30 a.m. and stagger to bed. Tears slide from my eyes as I cry myself to sleep. A cement block of grief presses my head to the pillow. When the alarm honks and hollers, I reel on Jell-O legs into the kitchen to begin the bread, reset the alarm for ninety minutes later, and crawl back into bed beside my sleeping husband. Sobs involuntarily shake from me, and Rich pulls me to himself, alert to my pain.

Just hours before, our friend was alive, playing tennis with his buddy. He'd cheered his dad at a triathlon, wondering if his own training would lend itself to such rigorous competition.

Just the day before, he had laughed with his brother and teased his mother as he solicitously cared for her after major surgery. He thought that maybe after getting his master's degree, he might use his fluent Spanish to get a job as a janitor, becoming an advocate for the downtrodden.

He was so alive.

No one expected death. We all expected life. He was young, vibrant, brilliant, with a soft heart for the underprivileged. He had given away his furniture, preferring a simple mattress on the floor and crates for his clothing. After working among orphaned and poverty-line children in Europe, he returned to America, sold his car, and rode a bike. His future was bright with hope and possibility, and in his path he strewed generous, burgeoning life.

In the program from his memorial service, he's pictured straddling two boulders with water rushing behind him, foaming and green as it crashes down the stream. His family inscribed, graffiti-style, on the foremost rock, "Peace."

Drew stood for peace, reconciliation, life amidst death—and too much dying.

Today I squint into the sun, surprised to see it perched so optimistically in the blue sky. Surrounded by the darkness of death, the brightness reminds me that life continues.

Death on the Way, by the Way

The great inevitable—death—always lurks just behind the door, skulking along the byways of our days. Some things never change.

Picture this: Jesus is walking about, coaching and coaxing life from those around him, speaking life into their hearts. He challenges the death warrant of sin and ultimately cancels it altogether. Before that, though, toward the end of Christ's ministry on earth, friends who know and love him send a frightened message: "Lord, behold, he whom You love is sick" (John 11:3).

Jesus responds without flurry and panic. He measures his answer carefully: "This sickness is not to end in death, but for the glory of God, so that the Son of God may be glorified by it" (verse 4). Not only does Jesus not race out the door and sprint the miles between him and his sick friend, he waits.

He waits two days before heading off and tells his disciples, "Our friend Lazarus has fallen asleep; but I go, so that I may awaken him out of sleep" (verse 11). Christ's followers find this comforting: *Whew. Well, then, if he's just asleep, he'll wake up soon and recover. Be good as new after a little sleep.*

Jesus's blunt answer to that line of thought destroys their comfort: "Lazarus is dead" (verse 14). Sure sounds like the real thing to me, like this sickness ended in death after all.

By the time Jesus finally arrives in Bethany, his friend is quite dead. He has inhabited the tomb for four days. The body already decays, the stench escapes the grave clothes and swarms behind the stone sealing the cave. Word of Jesus's approach travels to the mourning crowd, and Martha, Lazarus's sister, rushes to find him.

In her breathlessness, she confronts Jesus. "Lord, if You had been here, my brother would not have died" (verse 21). I like her *chutzpah:* "Where were you? What took you so long? Lazarus wouldn't be dead. He'd be alive and laughing and waiting for me to serve tuna pitas." I like, too, that Jesus is okay with this. He doesn't banish her for accusing him, in undertones, between the lines, of blowing the gig, of failing to deliver.

But Martha also summons faith to the fore: "Even now I know

that whatever You ask of God, God will give You" (verse 22). Whether she earnestly believes this in the core of her being or simply says words that repeat Christ's teaching, she nevertheless speaks truth.

Sometimes we must speak truth even if we aren't sure we believe it and aren't at all sure we can live in it. Sometimes we embrace what we know without feeling it in our hearts because we know the One who said it in the first place. Sometimes we refute our doubts, refuse the death around us, and speak living truth, even if the words seem dry and dusty and yellowed with age from storage in the attic of our soul.

Life Out of Death

Jesus's calm words of truth cut through the emotional chaos cluttering our soul—chaos that accompanies death, unexpected or expected: "Your brother will rise again" (verse 23).

And then, the words that steal the wind from our lungs and pump hope again into our hearts: "I am the resurrection and the life; he who believes in Me will live even if he dies, and everyone who lives and believes in Me will never die" (verses 25–26).

Live and believe in Jesus. Never die. Live even if we die. I could hear these words again and again, an unending refrain, until they pulse in my bloodstream, life itself, and fuel my every step, form my every thought.

I imagine then that in response to Jesus's words, the bees hold their breath, the breeze hushes, the chattering birds fall mute. Weeping and wailing cease. Silence like a scythe cuts the air. They are in the presence of the Creator of life.

Death is never wasted, though we may not see its redemption this side of the soil. Jesus tells the disciples, when they're still waiting for their cue to start the journey toward Lazarus, when they worry about returning to the place where Jesus recently escaped stoning, "I am glad for your sakes that I was not there, so that you may believe" (verse 15). Somehow, from Lazarus's death will come greater belief.

So it is with our deaths: the big deaths, the tragic losses of people and loves; the smaller deaths of jobs, homes, relationships. Somehow, out of the death, belief is possible. God wrings good out of every situation, however horrific. Life. The Shoot of Jesse will bring life.

An Appropriate Response

Does this mean that in the face of death we pull a stiff upper lip? that at death's doorbell, we smile and say, "So be it"? that when the lights go out, we whistle a happy tune? Perhaps burst into a few rousing rounds of "It is well, it is well, with my soul"?

To move too quickly from pain to praise ridicules the grief process and the volume of pain involved in loss. Mary and Martha seem angry at Lazarus's death, and both tell Jesus, "If you'd been here, this wouldn't have happened." Anger reflects the agony of living in a damaged, dying world. But anger must lead to sorrow. The crowd's reaction to Lazarus's death is weeping. Mary weeps. And Jesus's heart is troubled at their pain and their loss. He trembles with grief and agony; his spirit is stirring, agitated. The groaning wells up from deep within. And he weeps.

He weeps. The Lord of the Universe, the Word who spoke the world into being, weeps. For his friend's death and for death in general. He came to defeat death, and right in front of him, clothed in mourning's drab colors, lies the fallout of a fractured world—a world that was shattered at the entrance of the first two humans, a world that even now waits and groans for life in the midst of its death.

Jesus weeps.

And so we weep.

This is an appropriate response to death. We must create space for grieving, for mourning what has been lost and what that loss has cost us. Something is wrong if there are no tears. Through tears, our souls acknowledge that this is not what we were meant for. We were intended for Eden, for heaven, for a place with no tears and no sorrows, where death never touched a toe.

Noticing Death

But here, death abounds. I was young when a bright friend said, "Right now, your body is dying." I looked at my flesh, firm and sound, and refused to believe him. "No, Jane. Really. From the moment you're born, you start to die."

Physiologically, I guess this is so. But in between birth and death is a whole lot of living, though we don't always notice the living. Some just notice the dying: the bad news, the harsh relationship, the rupture in a child's life, the headlines and horrors of a world long lost from its moral pinning.

But spiritually, we often pretend that there is no death. That bad things don't happen to people who believe. And when they do, we are dumbfounded; we haven't a clue how to handle it, how to notice and honor another person living in a death-and-dying place. Sometimes we even refuse to allow wounded people to serve in strategic places in our churches, because erroneously we believe the lie that you have to be perfect to be a leader, that messy people shouldn't be leaders.

Au contraire. I'd take twelve broken people over twelve thousand people who have never faced their brokenness. That's what Jesus did: he took twelve sinners, people who abandoned him, cowered in fear, jostled for positions of priority, and he turned them into a team that changed the world.

We must notice death. Until we notice death, we will not know that we need life. We will never hear Jesus's next command.

Moving the Stone

Jesus, once more deeply moved, proceeds to the tomb. The pain roils up within him, and he orders, "Remove the stone."

Martha, the first to react, protests. "Lord, by this time there will be a stench, for he has been dead four days" (verse 39).

Probably Jesus knows this. But we do protest when our stones roll away. Their absence reveals our skeletal soul, our death rags. Stones help cork the stench, blocking out death and decay. Stones protect us, protect our death, keep out the light, lock in the dark.

We need someone to help move the stones. Jesus didn't move the stone himself, and neither did Lazarus. Instead, Jesus appointed someone else to do the work that could be done with human hands. Who will help move your stones? This is no task for a dead woman. This is a task for a friend, a friend not afraid of stench, not afraid of decay, not worried about the deterioration of soul and spirit and body that comes from living in this world.

That's a friend. If you must be dead in a cave, make sure you have a friend posted at the stone of your heart to roll it away at the right time.

And so they remove the stone. Jesus raises his eyes to heaven and invites God to hasten belief in those who will see his next move. This will be no wine from water miracle. He cries out with a loud voice, "Lazarus, come forth."

Come forth! Come out of death; come into life.

Lazarus recognizes the voice of Jesus calling, the voice of his friend. From deep inside his death place, Lazarus hears. Life quickens within. Lazarus hears Jesus calling him from outside his tomb, outside his grave clothes—"Lazarus, come forth."

He recognizes his Savior's voice. The resurrection and the life calls.

And the dead man walks

Out of death.

Into life.

God Help Me

The name *Lazarus* is the Greek version of *Eleazar*, meaning "God is my helper."

Lazarus stumbled from the tomb on dead-man's legs with God's strength helping him. And we are all Lazarus, each resurrected from the dead, raised into life.

This is Jesus calling. Jesus inviting you, inviting me, to live God-help-me lives as we move out of death into life, out of darkness into light. This is Jesus, naming us and reclaiming us from a living death and inviting us into abundant life. Come forth! And the way we live our lives—our living and believing in Christ—means that we, live only with God as our helper.

Jesus calls out, Lazarus, come forth—not to live in tombs, wrapped in death or in don'ts or to-dos—but calling you out, blinking into the brightness of a love so great that death dies.

Unbind Him

With strips of linen wound around his body, a square cloth tight about his head, and spices stuffed into all the layers, Lazarus's response to the Voice of Life is astounding. He lurches to his feet—does he lumber like the Tin Man, stiff and creaky?—and moves to the cave's entrance, moves toward life. Despite all the restrictions of death, all the trappings of grief, Lazarus heads back into life.

The crowd—mouths open, eyes open, hearts opening—gasps. Weeping and sorrow cease, replaced by wide-eyed wonder. Again, silence probably reigns, like heat-seared calm right after lightning, before thunder roars an answer. Jesus says, "Unbind him, and let him go" (verse 44).

Who can you call to your side to help unwind the grave clothes, the bindings and wrappings of death?

For years my covenant group's primary business, it seems, has been to help me unwrap those bindings, pull away those trappings, exposing new life. It's a little like spring at every meeting, like when I wade outside at the first sign of warmth and begin peeling back layers and layers of mulch and old slimy leaves, and underneath are fresh green pokes of life. My friends help unbind me.

They ask gentle questions or present a calm statement that I consider for a time, pray over, and invite God's truth to become apparent. When the odor from a death began to swell behind a stone in my soul, Karen offered to sit with me and listen, to reflect with me and ask questions prior to a personal retreat. When I am tempted to focus on another's part in my life, Linda or Sibyl or Adele will ask, "But what about you, Jane? What about how you are living there?" (Or dying there.)

Marilyn, her hands soft from years of tending bruised reeds, cupped my face last month and tenderly said, "I think you have made a decision you aren't aware of making. It may be okay, but look at that, if that is where you mean to be going." And throughout the tenure of our group, they have said, "You have been saying this for so long. What will be different this time?"

They help me unbind the grave clothes, help me to see the tender life beneath winter's death. They call me back to the resurrection and the life.

Who will help you unbind the trappings and set you free to hasten, stumbling, toward the Voice of Life? We must surround ourselves with people who beckon life. And we need to become life-beckoning women.

If you are still, if you sit within the bondage of death, what exactly are those bindings in your life? What reactions have you trapped yourself within, like some miserable *Groundhog Day* movie? What have you believed about yourself or about others that keeps you in bondage? What in your past forces the sprout of life in your heart back into the dark tomb, over and over? Listen to God call-ing you:

"God is my helper, come forth.

Unbind her, and let her go."

Reaction

Would that everyone cheered and applauded, praised God, and was transformed that day into Christ followers. Would that such a dra-matic deed—a dead man brought back to life!—created such a swell of new life that the entire world converted from death to life, moved over to the resurrection.

But not everyone celebrates when someone rises from the dead. Certainly they didn't with Lazarus: *How dare Jesus raise people from the dead?*

It's hard to believe that people would be angered by resurrection, that they wouldn't completely turn their hearts toward their true home, but they don't. Many did cheer and follow Christ, whether for Christ's sake or in order to see Lazarus, but "the chief priests planned to put Lazarus to death also; because on account of him many of the Jews were going away and were believing in Jesus" (John 12:10–11).

Crazy. You're raised from the dead and get a price on your head. Your life will mess with their minds, and faith, their preconceived notions and blocks. When God sets you free from your death, when you stagger from the tomb and friends unwrap the linen strips, not every guest seeing the spectacle will be supportive. Whatever your resurrection—healing old wounds, banishing depression, new life in relationships, a rebuilt dream, a new joy—when you change in re-sponse to life, the people around you will also change.

Your life forces them to question their own choices, to reevaluate their own encounters with—or avoidances of—the Author of life.

And their experience of your resurrection, of life coming forth from death, challenges them in their own death places, in the dark caves of their heart, where pain turns to rotting stench.

People will fight against the life in you.

Hold fast to that life. And pray for those who do not want to careen from their cave and learn to dance in new life, who do not want to dance the victory jig where life wins out over death. Don't lose hope for them. At their deepest level, their greatest longing battles with their greatest fear, but Christ can triumph, as he did with you.

Reclaiming Life

Jesus will always bring life out of death. It is his name: the One who saves, the resurrection and the life. Remember? "I came that they may have life...abundantly" (John 10:10). That life may not fit your tight definition. It may not look like eradication of cancer, a healed marriage, the spouse of your dreams, the return of the prodigal, or an unblemished life in a pockmarked planet. Please, don't be like the people who doubt Jesus because he doesn't heal the way they think he should. Cling to his words; cling to him.

We grip the hem of Christ's cloak when we repeat the truths we find in Scripture, such as, "They meant it for evil, but God means it for good, for the saving of many lives" (see Genesis 50:20), or "Your power is made perfect in my weakness" (see 2 Corinthians 12:9), or "You will never leave me or forsake me" (see Hebrews 13:5). We grab on to Jesus's hand when we remember who he is: the One who raises the dead. The One who, because *he* was raised from the dead, can raise us from our deaths.

Surveying the yard from my office window as I move from donated desk to hand-me-down recliner, I breathe deeply and take in: the green grass, the blooming purples of the ancient lilacs, the magenta of the redbuds, the pink-white blossoms of the apple trees. It's a resurrection day.

But I look beyond the beauty, knowing that beneath the rooflines of the homes around me, just as in our home, death sometimes reigns.

I raise my hand. Tears tremble along the rims of my eyes as I consider that death: troubled marriages, hurting teens, grieving parents, stumbling young adults. I recognize that death and call out life.

Come forth! Come forth in that home, in that heart. Come forth in hope, in a new direction, in a smile, a laugh, a restful sleep, a quickening of love.

Come forth.

Thank you, Jesus. You alone have the words of life. Where else would we go?

    • come and consider •

From deep inside the binds of death,
A quickening.
A response to a voice you know,
A voice calling your name,
"Lazarus, come forth!"
Come out of death.
Come out of darkness.
Discard the grave clothes that wrap the decay.

He who breathed life into the first Adam,
The first Eve,
Now waits to breathe life into you.
Fill your lungs with that life, let Christ
Speak to your dead places,
Unwrap the cloths that bind you.

What will Jesus call forth in you?
Where is there death?
Remember, remember:
"Even if he dies, he will live again."
And so it is with you, your heart,
Your soul,
The harsh, dead, decaying tombs of
Your past and your present.
Even though parts of you have died,
You will live again.
Because Jesus said,
"I am."
"I am the resurrection and the life."
He is. And so you, too,
Come forth.

• come for life •

I am the resurrection and the life; he who believes in Me will live even if he dies, and everyone who lives and believes in Me will never die. Do you believe this?

John 11:25–26

• come closer •

- Take time to notice death in your life. Where is it? When was there no one to mourn with you? Where were you disappointed that Jesus did not come sooner, did not respond the way you hoped?
- Who in your life helps roll away the stone, unwrap the bindings of the grave clothes?

- Where do you long for life? What great fear is battling with your greatest longing? What is the fear about?
- When do people resist the life you represent? Who fights against life in you?
- Where do you live into the name "God is my helper?"

• come home •

Oh God,
These clothes constrict me,
choke me,
bind the very life in me.
Call me out;
bring me into the light and into the life.
Please. Help me unbind those trappings
and breathe in the
resurrection and the life.
You have called me,
and I come
on trembling legs
into your light.
Thank you,
my resurrection,
my life.
Amen.

• come today •

How will you come forth today from death?

come,
follow me

"Looking at him, Jesus felt a love for him
and said to him,'...come, follow Me.'"
—Mark 10:21

• • • • •

Come, Almighty to deliver,
    Let us all Thy life receive;
    Suddenly return and never,
    Nevermore Thy temples leave.
    Thee we would be always blessing,
    Serve Thee as Thy hosts above,
    Pray and praise Thee without ceasing,
    Glory in Thy perfect love.
                CHARLES WESLEY

One Saturday morning, I was lurking around the bakery down-
town. Only once in a while did they bake my favorite, salt-
rising bread, and I hoped today was my lucky day. While I waited,
mewing lured me away from the bakery to the alley where I tracked
down the mournful sound. At age ten, my emotions won most battles.

The bakery lost its appeal when I saw the kitten, thin as a stick, looking like it had bathed in an oil spill. Probably crawling with diseases, it surely hadn't eaten any food in a long time.

Who can resist such a waif?

After strong resistance to my pleading, the cat finally tiptoed close enough to sniff my fingers, then rasped its tongue over their tips. I nabbed it and carried it home. Scratch marks on my arms belied my opening line:

"Look, Mom! See what followed me home?"

The flip reminded me of competition swimmers. The turn-around time clocked about three seconds: "March yourself right back to that alley with that cat."

Following is a decision of the will. The cat did not follow me home. I had locked it in my bony arms and forced it.

Jesus will never do this to us. We elect to follow him. And if we want to have life, real life—abundant life—and if we want to reach the source of our underground longings, it's an easy decision.

Follow Me

"Good Teacher, what shall I do to inherit eternal life?" The rich young man in Mark 10 races up to Jesus and kneels before him, bowing to Jesus's authority.

Running doesn't seem very dignified for a man of his wealth, but what a breathtaking picture of his need.

Jesus is taking off on another journey, crowds of people trailing along behind him. But he stops, comments on the man's word "good," and then recites some of the commandments: don't murder, don't commit adultery, don't steal, don't lie, don't defraud, honor your father and mother.

From his kneeling position, the man says, "Teacher, I have kept all these things from my youth up." In other words, "I'm doing it all right, but it's not working. I don't feel very alive, and I sure don't know anything about eternal life. And if this is all there is, I'm in trouble."

Jesus looks at him, and his love launches his next words, "One thing you lack: go and sell all you possess and give to the poor, and you will have treasure in heaven; and come, follow Me" (Mark 10:17–21).

The scripture tells us, "But at these words he was saddened, and he went away grieving, for he was one who owned much property" (verse 22).

What was lacking?

The blessing of empty hands—hands that hold nothing but Jesus.

A Rule Follower

As a rule follower from way back, I can relate to the man's self-righteousness. He did everything right, kept all the commandments Jesus listed. But it's a hollow existence, squishing out joy and eliminating faith. I crossed my *t*'s, dotted my *i*'s, obeyed teachers and tried not to lie (sometimes that didn't work so well). I tried to be nice and stay quiet. But my motives were not so that I could be like Jesus. My legalism was about being liked, being safe: *If I follow the rules, I won't get in trouble, and maybe everyone will be happy.*

Self-righteous people aren't the happiest people I've ever encountered, myself included. They aren't much fun to be around. Other people who don't follow the rules drive us nuts, and it's hard to tolerate them, let alone love them (which was one of the rules Jesus didn't recite for the rich young man). We tend to get caught up with doing things right rather than focusing on the relationships around us. And we can be a tad judgmental.

Rule followers want to be right and want to establish or maintain control. Self-control is the bare minimum we desire, with controlling others as a follow-up agenda.

Jesus wasn't inviting this man to follow more rules. Rules are predictable.

Jesus was inviting this man to abandon all the rules, all the things that made him feel comfortable and in control of his life, and to follow him. There's a big difference. Salvation does not come from amassing wealth or from rule keeping.

Not to say that we should break the rules and sin, sin, sin. Our obedience comes from loving Jesus so much, from loving his loving of us, that we don't want to do anything to separate ourselves from him or rupture that relationship. But keeping the rules doesn't mean you're following Jesus. Obedience is good and not sinning is important, but the source of our obedience is our love for Jesus, and the source of our strength is Jesus.

God's ultimate rule—"Be holy as I am holy" (see Leviticus 19:2)—taken out of context could lead us to rule-following for salvation. But the scripture goes on to say, "I am the LORD, who makes you holy" (Leviticus 22:32, NIV). God makes us holy. Holiness cannot be attained without Christ's life, death, and resurrection.

What Stops Us from Following

The man in our story learned this. The Message version of Mark 10:22 reads, "The man's face clouded over. This was the last thing he expected to hear, and he walked off with a heavy heart. He was holding on tight to a lot of things, and not about to let go."

We're all like this fellow in some way. He held on to his money, status, and lifestyle; he had a lot of the rules right. But he missed the essentials. What he held on to held him hostage.

What do you hold, what do you clutch, that is not Jesus?

Is it a boyfriend? Do you tell yourself that it's okay because you love each other and you both love Jesus while a suspicion wiggles inside you? Does loving your man keep you from loving Jesus fully?

Maybe you put your husband, or your hopes for a husband, above your love for God and are constantly distracted from your first love?

Or maybe you clutch your children. Are they your life? Do you wrap yourself in their sports and music lessons and grades and appearances, believing that you look better when they succeed? Do you live vicariously through them? Do you try to control them, manipulating their schedules and futures so that you can feel good about yourself or make up for your own broken dreams?

Your clutching will kill you. It won't help your relationships either.

Or maybe you glom on to your possessions: your prestigious home, designer clothes, great car, or that megagrill parked on the patio. Or do your supersized toys, your resort trips, or your career demand your heart and soul?

Perhaps that's not you at all. You have high standards, and you give a decent amount of money away to your church with every paycheck. You follow the rules, volunteer for the nursery and the homeless shelter, and attend the Bible study each week.

Is it your role? Maybe you're the perfect wife and homemanager. You keep up your appearance and appearances, smile at the right times, play "happy hostess," iron the shirts, do the laundry, keep your home immaculate. You never make waves, never ask for more passion or more hope or more laughter.

Or not. One friend clutches her pain like an oxygen tank. She needs that pain so she doesn't have to change, doesn't have to grow, doesn't have to forgive. Her pain provides an excuse not to risk. Another clenches ambition in alligator jaws. To let go means giving up, so she holds on, fighting for the next promotion, the next project.

Still not you? Are you proud of being a nonconformist? No one controls you, nothing clutches you. You are free, easy, and take life in stride. Everything is fine, just fine. Is that not clinging?

What do you grip in your fist?

Where are you fist boxing your way through your days, your life?

What "Follow Me" Means

When Jesus says, "Follow me," don't think clothes made with camel's hair, white robes, self-flagellation, rules and regulations, and giving up all creature comforts.

In *Young Frankenstein,* a spoof on the original monster movies, Igor greets a visitor at the door. Igor is hunchbacked with a pronounced limp. "Walk this way," he growls and hobbles into the hallway. The guest, looking puzzled, imitates Igor's gait, lurching and dragging one of his legs behind him.

"Walk this way." That's all Jesus means. Walk the way he did. If the young man, with all his worldly goods, trailed after Jesus, what would the man see?

In the next verses and chapters, Jesus works with his disciples on the whole idea raised by the encounter with the wealthy man ("Who can be saved, then, if it's impossible for the rich to inherit the kingdom of God?"). Jesus predicts his own death in a painful, haunting conversation. When two disciples (and their mother!) accost him with a self-centered request—"Teacher, we want You to do for us whatever we ask of You" (Mark 10:35)—Christ says, "What do you want Me to do for you?" He already knows but wants to give them enough rope to trip themselves. Their goal to sit at the right and left hands of Jesus in glory is sickening in its context of his prediction of his death. Still, Jesus responds without recrimination.

Then he says, "Whoever wishes to become great among you shall be your servant; and whoever wishes to be first among you shall be slave of all. For even the Son of Man did not come to be served, but to serve, and to give His life a ransom for many" (Mark 10:43–45).

The root word for *follow* literally means "road," and when they hit the road for Jericho—remember, Jesus was setting out for a journey when the rich man ran up to him—he heals the blind Bartimaeus and then climbs the hill toward Jerusalem. He climbs to his own death.

That is some road.

He loves people. He works with them. He teaches them, heals them, forgives them. He serves them. He dies for them. He buys them back from their hostage to sin and gives them life.

On the Road

When Jesus saw the first couple of men who would become his disciples, they were fishing. They'd been fishing all night, in fact, and kept drawing up a gaping, dripping net, full of holes and empty of fish. Jesus climbed into one of the boats, asked the guys to row him out a bit, and started teaching the multitudes.

Then he said, "Put out into the deep water and let down your nets for a catch" (Luke 5:4). Peter, who owned the boat, probably thought Jesus was nuts. "Master, we worked hard all night and caught nothing, but I will do as You say and let down the nets" (verse 5).

They caught so many fish that their newly repaired nets began to break.

No wonder when Jesus said, "Follow Me, and I will make you fishers of men," in Matthew's telling of the story, they followed him. Got on the same road.

What were Jesus's words to the rich young man, the rule-keeping man with many possessions? "One thing you lack: go and sell all you possess and give to the poor, and you will have treasure in heaven; and come, follow Me." In all of our striving, achieving, seizing, and rule keeping, we overlook the impetus of Jesus's response to the wealthy, rule-keeping man: "Looking at him, Jesus felt a love for him" (Mark 10:21).

This is the rich man's lesson: hang on to Jesus, to the love he wants to pour into your heart (see Romans 5:5). Clutch his robe. Don't let him out of your sight. He is your life. Apart from him we can do nothing; we have nothing; we are nothing. Let nothing grow between you and him. Cling to him. Clinging to anything or anyone else means our hands aren't free to grab on to Jesus.

And this truth is ours too. To be really rich, we unclench our fists, open our hands, and reach for Jesus. He promised us life, abundant life, and we create room for that life when we let go.

Whatever is in your grip, recognize it. Notice why you hold that person, that role, that ambition, so tightly. Invite Christ to pry your fingers off those temporal prizes, and let him have you, all of you— your hopes for the future, your pain from the past, your roles and rules and relationships.

"Get on the road with me," Jesus says. "Don't put your stock in your stuff. Put it in me. I'm your real treasure."

Heaven someday?

No. Heaven today.

 • come and consider •

Come, follow me.
Walk in my footprints,
Dance in my arms.
Love as I love,
Live as I live.
Live in me.
Only through me
Will you really live.
In this world and
Through me you will

Have power to live well,
To love well,
To follow me.

• come for life •

Blessed be the God and Father of our Lord Jesus Christ, who has blessed us with every spiritual blessing in the heavenly places in Christ, just as He chose us in Him before the foundation of the world, that we would be holy and blameless before Him.

Ephesians 1:3–4

• come closer •

- Who are some rule followers you know? Are you one of them? How much stock do you really place in getting it right? How does that hurt or help you and your relationships?
- What does "follow me" mean to you? What stops you from following Jesus fully?
- In what ways do you live as though earth and its stuff were your real treasures instead of Christ?
- What do you clutch? What would faith look like in terms of letting go?
- How do you follow Christ? Where do you experience the "treasure in heaven" freedom?

• come home •

Father,
This scares me a bit,

to be honest with you.
I have a lot of stuff around me
that feels pretty good.
And the people I love,
and the activities I prize—
this gets a little scary when
I hear you say,
"Sell everything you possess."
Please,
take away my desire for anything
that outranks my desire for you.
Give me a longing for you
that is real,
as obvious as my heartbeat
or my breath on a cold winter's day.
Help me to clutch your hand
like I would wear my mittens
in the snow,
and warm me just that way
as I trust you
and set out yet again
on this journey
to your heart.
Amen.

• come today •

How will you come today and follow Jesus?

come
and see

"Rabbi...where are You staying?"
..."Come, and you will see."
John 1:38–39

· · · · ·

Come home, come home.
  You who are weary, come home;
  Earnestly, tenderly, Jesus is calling,
  Calling, O sinner, come home.
          WILL L. THOMPSON

The sun broils the grass, bleaching it to the color of straw. Our
neighbors invited a group of friends from work to their home
to play outside and do some team building. If our neighbors are like
us, they will have slaved to make all things ready for professional
friends to come by.

Having company is like putting your house on the market: a
showing of all the assets of your home, a hiding of all the defects. Years
ago, as a newlywed with a bad case of disorganization (it is a chronic
case, I must hasten to add, in case you plan to stop by), I was

impressed by my friend Bonnie's sign, which went something like this: IF YOU CAME TO SEE ME, WELCOME. IF YOU CAME TO SEE MY HOUSE, PLEASE MAKE AN APPOINTMENT.

When people I love move into a new place, whether an apartment or condo or town home or house, I want to see where they live, but not to critique it. I love helping them move. I want to see them in their home, so that if we talk on the phone while they are cooking, I can envision them in the kitchen. I can picture them reading in the overstuffed chairs with their purple and red pillows, or sitting at the computer, or putting clothes in the closet. Context is important to me as a writer and as a woman with a nesting instinct.

And I love having people over to our home pretty much. But the list of people I trust to step without judgment over all our stuff—flip-flops and stray socks, the gardening gloves and muddy shoes, the orange backpack and the lacrosse stick, the hockey bag and the Frisbee, the jackets and discarded sweatshirt, a satchel left from a trip and a stack of library books (probably overdue)—is pretty short. And that just gets you in the living room door. You should see the dining room table.

I love hospitality, but I have more important things to do than housework. And if I invite you to my home, it is not to showcase our modest dwelling. That would take more than even deep cleaning. It would require complete gutting and starting over, and someone else's budget and time and skills.

No, an invitation for those trusted few to come in is an invitation to feel welcome, but also an invitation to accept us as we are: a busy, messy family with busy, messy lives. With Jesus, however, the invitation to come in is an invitation to an abundant, forever life.

Come, and You Will See

John's and Jesus's mothers were pregnant together: Elizabeth, far past childbearing age, and Mary, a young teenager. Mary ran to Elizabeth,

her cousin, after the angel announced to Mary that she would be the
mother of the Christ, the One to bring light into the world's night.
When Mary entered Elizabeth's home, John leaped in his mother's
womb because he recognized Jesus's presence.

And now, fast-forward some thirty years. Yesterday, Jesus passed
by and John again recognized him as the Christ, the Messiah. John
stated with conviction, after baptizing Jesus, "I myself have seen,
and have testified that this is the Son of God" (John 1:34). John
had called out, "I am a voice of one crying in the wilderness,
'Make straight the way of the Lord,' as Isaiah the prophet said"
(John 1:23).

Today, John the Baptizer stands with two of his disciples, and
again sees Jesus. He has spent his adult life preparing the way for
Christ, inviting people into repentance, tutoring them as disciples.
Now, Christ comes. Christ is present, moving among them.

Eternity walks into the dust of their daily lives.

John utters the only possible words: "Behold, the Lamb of God!"
(verse 36).

Two of John's students, who learned of the One who is to come,
hear John. Their feet are riveted to the ground, their gaze on Christ's
face. *Can it be? Is this true? The One we have been proclaiming has broken into humanity and brought hope into our despair?*

The Message catches the thrill of this coming:

The Word became flesh and blood,
    and moved into the neighborhood.
We saw the glory with our own eyes,
    the one-of-a-kind glory,
    like Father, like Son,
Generous inside and out,
    true from start to finish. (John 1:14)

Wordless, the two men leave John's side and follow Jesus.

Jesus turns, sees them following Him. He asks, pointedly, "What do you seek?" (see John 1:37–39).

"Rabbi (which translated means Teacher), where are You staying?"

"Come, and you will see."

Their world is about to shift.

Seeing Is Believing

What does it mean to see, to really see, to have our eyes opened? What does it cost us? I love it that Jesus heals the blind—the physically unseeing—not just once or twice but throughout his earthly ministry. And isn't it interesting that the visually impaired often recognized him first, often before those with sight.

To really see is to invite God to scrape away our cataracts—the beliefs that distort our vision, the questions we have about God and Scripture and faith, the idolatrous thinks we think of God. Those cataracts make God in our own image—we'll believe in Jesus if he acts the way we think he should. Show me first, God. Then I'll believe. Faith takes a backseat when we demand a visual demo.

Even Jesus said, "Blessed are they who did not see, and yet believed" (John 20:29). How hard is it to go along with what your eyes see? He's asking us to believe without seeing—to come and then see.

Jesus's invitation, "Come, and you will see," is an invitation to faith.

And Scripture tells us, "Now faith is the assurance of things hoped for, the conviction of *things not seen*" (Hebrews 11:1, emphasis mine). The writer continues, "And without faith it is impossible to please Him, for he who comes to God must believe that He is and that He is a rewarder of those who seek Him" (verse 6).

Where is faith required of you right now? What impossibilities lie before you, what implausibilities confront you? Make a list of those places: the prodigal child, the unemployed husband, the hateful colleague, the mother who never approves of you, or the father who abandoned you but now needs you.

Jesus doesn't demand anything of us that he isn't willing to provide. The author of Hebrews goes on to tell us that Jesus is "the author and perfecter of faith" (Hebrews 12:2), and we are to fix our eyes on him. When Jesus fills our eyes, when we see, really see him, impractical faith makes perfect sense.

An Invitation

The law of inertia states that "an object at rest will remain at rest unless acted upon by an external and unbalanced force. An object in motion will remain in motion unless acted upon by an external and unbalanced force." Jesus's invitation exerted an outside force on the lives of those men, and the lives of all they encountered, that would change the world.

Jesus also asks all who follow him into honesty: "What do you seek?"

This is a good question. A lot of people followed Jesus then (and follow him now) because he passed out goodies right and left. They wanted the toys from the parade, the candy from the floats, and the foam footballs that politicians lobbed into the crowd. And wouldn't a miracle or two be nice, as well?

When I first came to Christ as a teenager, no one asked, "What do you seek? What do you expect when you come to Christ?"

Hope wasn't part of my college vocabulary. But if I could have verbalized my hope, I think I hoped for relief from buried pain and some life terrain that was a little softer than the limestone gravel I tended to race over barefoot. Maybe a presto-change-o magic to reverse my awkwardness, make me a social fit instead of a misfit, give me the right words to say at the right time instead of silences that gaped like missing teeth. A boyfriend would be nice, too—someone less like an octopus and more like a real man.

As I made that list just now and reread it, God's goodness hushes me. I can hardly lift my face to him as I realize that, one by one, he has met all those unspoken, unhoped for hopes. Sure, pain still litters our world, like pottery chips poking through the grass. We will get cut when we walk about. And I contribute to the danger with my own fractured parts.

These were not overnight miracles. No magic acts here. But slowly, now years later, life blooms where once death reeked. I am still shy but am learning that silence isn't bad. Silence gives others space to think, to breathe, and to feel and speak instead of my cutting off their words. I have a good and patient husband who puts up with the sharps that poke through once in a while. And God is recycling, redeeming old pain through my writing and speaking and individual relationships. When the outside force that is Jesus Christ acted upon my life, he rocked me from my roots and set me in motion. I cannot thank him enough.

What do you seek?

If you seek a Savior, you've looked in the right place. Welcome.

An Invitation to Intimacy

"What do you seek?" I love the disciples' answer: we want to know where you live. It expresses a longing for intimacy, for a deeper knowing. Inviting someone home means inviting them to accept us. When the two disciples asked Jesus, "Where do you live?" they were not asking an idle question.

If this man is truly the Messiah, then the disciples will see it in his life, in his lifestyle, in his home. "Where do you live? Are you grounded in reality? Do your words match your home and lifestyle? What is your life like?"

Jesus doesn't maintain a safe distance. He takes the men home with him. Wherever home is. The Scriptures are taciturn about a building with four walls that Jesus calls home. We know he lived with his parents growing up, but later he says, "The foxes have holes and the birds of the air have nests, but the Son of Man has nowhere to lay His head" (Luke 9:58).

So where do the disciples go when Jesus says, "Come, and you will see"? Where do they have supper, where do they sleep, where is Jesus's home?

I think it is in heaven, and the disciples are invited to experience not the life of a transient, a homeless person pushing around a cart of belongings, but the heart of someone who came from heaven and who waits to take us there with him.

An Invitation to Acceptance

When a guest enters our home, no matter who they are, we beckon them not just into the building we inhabit, but into a portion of our lives, as much as we are willing or able to share with them. Christ's words, "Come and see," were also an invitation to accept him, accept his life, accept his calling. "Take me, take my life."

They have no idea where Jesus really lives, no idea about his motto, his theme verse, his mission statement so popular in organizations today. All that these men know is what John said: "This was He of whom I said, 'He who comes after me has a higher rank than I, for He existed before me'" (John 1:15).

John's followers likely were with John when Jesus came seeking baptism. They saw heaven's curtain swing wide, saw the Holy Spirit descend like a dove, heard the Father's voice, "You are My beloved Son, in You I am well-pleased" (Luke 3:22).

Well, that's a pretty powerful introduction.

Christ, when he says, "Come, and you will see," invites the disciples to be part of his life. And in so doing, says as well, "I accept you as my guests." This is a risky acceptance for us human hosts. I want people to discard shoes at the door, be careful with our hardwood floors, not leave rings of moisture on the antique furniture. And if I have just scrubbed those hardwood floors (which has happened twice in seven years, both times in honor of our older children's high school graduations), I may well put a sign on the door requesting the shoe drop. Not the nicest welcome sign, perhaps.

One of those two disciples is called a "son of thunder." Now there's a hearty calling card. If you know that someone who crashes around is coming over, you put away all your china and the crystal candy bowl and the fragile baby cradle that was your great-grandmother's. With a nickname like that, do you want him coming over to play with your child? Young Thunder would break all the toys.

But Jesus just says, "Come."

Think back to all the places where you have not been welcomed, not been honored, not been loved. Now superimpose Jesus's words over those old messages: "I accept you," he says. "I love you. I receive you as my guest. Come and see."

Come As You Are

In college, sometimes we'd pound on doors and drag friends to a "come as you are" party. If they were in a tank top and cut-offs, or studying for an exam, or gorging on pizza, or blow-drying their hair, they came. Whether they had on their jammies or had just been running, they came. Whatever their state of repair, or more likely disrepair, they came.

What if this were the case in our churches? If we didn't expect people to come all cleaned up, spit shined and pressed, with mouthwash freshening their breath? What if someone weaves into the church with alcohol seeping through her pores? What if a wife shows up with a black eye? What if a drug addict plops down in the front row? Or someone who forgot their antipsychotics that morning?

Can we say, "Come as you are"?

Can we really issue the same invitation that Christ offers, "Come and see"? Come and see who Jesus is, based on how we receive you in church today. Come and see who Jesus is, given the way I treat you in Sunday school or at the grocery store. Come and see what this life is all about, this life that Jesus offers. May our churches someday be the safest place in the world for people who need healing—healing from emotional pain, from old wounds, from ruptured relationships. They will see love and acceptance in our eyes, and then they will meet the Jesus who puts those qualities in us. The world churns out wounded people; may we offer the balm of Gilead to those who come to church, who seek hope and help from the Messiah, those who seek healing and life. Abundant life.

When we have seen, really seen, where Jesus lives, when we have moved in with him and he with us, then our life begins to change. He sees our innards, knows where ugliness hides or disapproval lurks or perfectionism rules. And he begins a house cleaning, an ongoing ridding out. We begin to look, little by little, like Jesus. We may even begin to sound like him.

After spending the day with him, the disciples convert to Jesus's path. Immediately Andrew finds his brother Simon and yanks him aside with the good news: "We have found the Messiah." Jesus changes Simon's name to Peter and on they go. The next day, Jesus finds Philip and says, "Follow Me."

See the pattern?

The next thing you know, Philip finds Nathanael. "We have found Him of whom Moses in the Law and also the Prophets wrote—Jesus of Nazareth, the son of Joseph" (John 1:45).

Nathanael asks, "Can any good thing come out of Nazareth?"

Philip challenges him with, "Come and see" (John 1:46). And the ripple effect continues, from those dusty days so long ago, until today, when we get to tell others, "I have found him. Come and see." Wouldn't it be wonderful if we could say, "Live with me, and you will see Jesus"?

Homecoming

In all of us there is a longing for home, for a real home, a safe place, a refuge from pain and betrayal, from disappointment and grief. A place where we are deeply loved no matter how we act, where we are nurtured and cheered on in our run for life. We look for this home in various concrete ways: the arms of family around us, walls and a roof with our name on the mailbox, an appreciative community at work, a loving spouse.

In the film *The Notebook,* Noah's wife, Allie, lives in an Alzheimer's unit. He spends as much time with her as possible, though she rarely breaks through the memory-stealing fog to recognize him. When the two gather with their family outside, their grown children say to Noah, "Come home with us. She doesn't know you."

He looks at them in surprise. "Your mother is my home."

Such a sweet, breath-stealing line. But when Allie dies, where does that leave Noah?

Homeless.

If we make our home anywhere but with Christ, our home will ultimately be destroyed. But if we "come and see," if we make our home in Christ, then wherever we are, Christ is. In an amazing, heavenly twist, a Jesus juxtaposition, when Christ bids us "Come and see," he also turns and asks, "Can I come in and live with you? Can I make your heart my home?"

When we say yes to his invitation, we say yes to a forever home. Imagine what that means as we live in our temporary homes. For Carol, it means welcoming others with the generous love of Christ: "Come in, come in! Have you had dinner? Would you like some juice?" For Shirley it means the kindest words you've ever heard coming straight from her heart. For all of us, it means that bit by bit, we become more interested in others than in our own convenience or inconvenience.

Might as well get out your WELCOME mat and take down the CLEAN FLOORS—REMOVE SHOES sign. Or at least change it to read, "Come and see."

• come and consider •

Come and see,
See my life, see my home,
See my heart for you,
My pain for your anguish,
My longing for your healing.
Come, see how I live,
Dine with me,
Move in with me.
Press your ear against my chest
And hear my heart.
Let me be your true home,
The place you've always longed for,

The love of your life.
And then, you will really
Live. Abundantly.
Please.
Come, and you will see.

• come for life •

I am the vine, you are the branches; he who abides in Me and I in
him, he bears much fruit, for apart from Me you can do nothing.…
Just as the Father has loved Me, I have also loved you; abide in My
love. If you keep My commandments, you will abide in My love; just
as I have kept my Father's commandments and abide in His love.

John 15:5, 9–10

• come closer •

- What did you seek when you first came to Christ? What do
  you seek when you come now?
- In your life, what has it meant to see? Where have you invited
  the Messiah to remove the cataracts? How did that impact
  your life? Where are you blinded now?
- When is faith the hardest for you? What questions or problems hinder your faith?
- Think back to all the places where you have not been welcomed, honored, loved. Now superimpose Jesus's words over
  those old messages: "I accept you. I love you. I receive you as
  my guest." What happens for you?
- If your heart really is Christ's home, how can you welcome
  others and invite them to "come and see"?

• come home •

Jesus,
When you invited me to come and see,
when you took me in, just as I am,
without a plea,
I had no idea. You came to me
and wooed me into your home.
You moved into the neighborhood of my heart—
in spite of questions, in spite of my unbelieving parts.
You love me.
You really, really love me.
Your love changes everything.
There's no place like home.
I hang a WELCOME *sign over my life.*
May many come
and see you.
In your saving name,
amen.

• come today •

How will you come today and see?

PART 2

.....

love
Relationships

come
for healing

"I will come and heal him."
—Matthew 8:7

• • • • •

Who is he that from the grave
Comes to heal and help and save?
'Tis the Lord, O wondrous story!
'Tis the Lord, the King of glory.
BENJAMIN HANBY

t felt like a body cast for the soul. Frozen, unable to reach forward or reach out, my heart immobilized by years of not trusting, not feeling, not talking. I could not muster the strength to retrain myself to love, to forgive, to even care. I played church; I read the Scripture; I knew the Lord Jesus as my Savior. But for too long, I had stuffed my wounds full of gauze to keep from bleeding all over others. The resultant poisoning paralyzed me.

When my emotional paralysis began to erode my marriage, to impact my small children, the timer rang. I had to either get going or get out.

I got going. "Lord Jesus, come and heal me," my heart cried.

But healing was not overnight. No whisk of a wand or wave of a hand. This kind of healing forced me to ask questions about this Jesus: Is he real? Does he heal? Does Christianity really work?

This healing required attending support groups every week for years, studying and living in the connection between soul growth and emotional health, and choosing day after day to do the hard work of trusting, talking, feeling. It meant tending to the wounds as they occurred rather than allowing them to fester, and always, always, it meant putting my relationship with Christ first.

Even now, years later, this is not natural behavior.

Somehow the world imprinted on my frontal lobes the message that life isn't safe and neither are relationships. Keeping my mouth quiet substituted for safety, though my moodiness damaged others. Eventually the anger burst through any self-imposed gag order, burning myself and others on blastoff.

But brains can be retrained. We do not have a God who is powerless over our concerns. Our God raised Jesus from the dead. Surely he can do the same for us in our various stages of unhealing and paralysis.

After a lifetime of feeling different from everyone else, and thus unacceptable, the first thing I learned at those meetings was, "You are not alone."

I dammed the tears pressing against my eyes as I looked around the table, heard the stories, and tasted honesty. "I'm not okay. I'm really pretty messed up. But that's okay because you are too. And we're together in this."

Though they may not know it, people all around us are paralyzed—paralyzed by pain, fear, rejection, abandonment, shattered dreams, disappointment, loss. Beginning at Eden's threshold, paralysis continues throughout time.

Jesus knew this, and as the most fully alive human being ever, he came to bring life to our limp limbs, withered hearts, and strait-jacketed souls. At every intersection, he encountered people who needed healing, deliverance, and freedom.

And the wounded? The hurting and scarred, bruised and battered, always worked their way to Christ. His demeanor and his actions showed his heart, and people paraded after him, hoping for help.

The Centurion

When Jesus enters Capernaum, hubbub follows. A crowd gathers, and a Roman officer runs toward the center of attention. Jesus's reputation precedes him, and this officer needs the miracle worker, the man who went about breathing life into a dying and desperate world. But the centurion, who oversees a hundred troops, isn't seeking his own well-being.

Finding Christ, he immediately lays out his need: "Lord, my servant is lying paralyzed at home, fearfully tormented" (Matthew 8:6). He doesn't beg for healing. Like an underling reporting to a high-ranking official, he states his problem. And waits.

The centurion, humbled by his servant's condition, seeks the Messiah, the One who rises from the dark shadows of a suffering planet with healing in his wings.

Jesus surveys the man: a Gentile, a leader. Christ already knows what others would tell him: the man's donations built the synagogue (see Luke 7:4–5), and he loves the Jewish nation. But Jesus peers below the surface and sees a man who cares about his servant, lying in great pain, immobilized.[1]

He doesn't wait for the centurion to ask. When Jesus sees, compassion follows. "I will come and heal him" (Matthew 8:7).

Only one slight problem: Jews were not allowed to associate with

Gentiles. They couldn't talk with them, eat with them, or visit in their homes. Thus, many people might have missed the good news, letting social constraints or restraints stop them from moving to the Savior who offers healing.

But this rule does not offend the officer nor deter him—he accepts the rule and bows to the ruler. "Lord, I am not worthy for You to come under my roof, but just say the word, and my servant will be healed" (verse 8). He recognizes what others did not: neither time nor space bind this Savior. The Messiah can heal anyone from any location.

And Jesus, blithely nondiscriminatory in his relationships and his healing, would dare to darken any door. He would gladly go to the centurion's home to heal the servant. Yet he pulls this thread from the warp and woof of the officer's soul: "Truly I say to you, I have not found such great faith with anyone in Israel" (verse 10).

That faith swung wide the door for Gentiles to share Jesus's offer of abundant life. But abundant life is a choice.

Catching Up, Growing Up

"This is so exasperating! I've never seen anything so inefficient in my life." Her white hair curled about her head, and she fussed and fumed as she dragged her luggage toward the elevator. En route she spewed a stream of frustration and anger.

I recognized her. We met last year, same time, same place: a gathering of Christian professionals. Evidently her attitude had not improved. She ranted and raved then, no doubt feeling justified in doing so. No bellhop waited to haul luggage from trunk to cart to room. The elevator was slow thirty years ago and showed no signs of revving its outdated engine for anyone's benefit. The situation frustrated anyone focused on problems rather than anticipating God's work at the conference.

But I also recognized her, eventually, in my own mirror. I was that woman, four decades down the road, gray headed and vitriolic. *One day I will be her age. What if I am just as angry, just as untamed, just as unformed as she?*

My husband, hearing of a celebrity couple's divorce, said, "I think he would be hard to live with—he doesn't strike me as someone who has caught up with his soul. He's not in tune with himself." The celebrity's self-awareness got checked at the door to fame, blocking recognition of his own issues, needs, blind spots, dysfunctions—just plain sin.

Looking at my journal entries of the past month, I realize I haven't caught up with myself either. My self-awareness factor logged in at zero. I spit venom about other people's behavior without recognizing my own sin. *Why don't they grow up?* I've fumed in writing. In all these recorded instances, I've failed to communicate well; I've acted like a six-year-old. My ragged, off-center soul has demanded perfection from others, and not myself. Though I dove after other folks, dragging them back into relationship with perfunctory apologies, my internal blame needle actually pointed at them and their problems.

Catch up with yourself. Where do you need to grow up? Where are you paralyzed? Where is there nerve apathy?

Part of catching up is figuring out how our paralysis benefits us. For instance, if you were paralyzed at emotional adolescence, and now when you blow up in anger, you get your way or get attention or get left alone, how does this get you what you really want? How can you discern your real and legitimate needs and longings, and get them met in adult-appropriate, Christlike ways?

That's catching up.

A Friend Who Intercedes

Soon after crossing paths with that woman at the convention, I wondered, *Doesn't she have friends and family? someone to love her and to reflect back to her where her ragged edges could use a little soothing, a touch of smoothing by the Savior? Does no one expect or encourage healing this side of heaven? Emotional, spiritual, physical? Or at least growth? Do people just flap their hands and say, "Oh well, that's the way she is. She'll never change"?*

Why don't our friends expect us to "get well"—to rise from all our deaths—to become more loving, patient, kind, good, joyful?

The Savior I know brings healing wherever he goes, if I'm open to receiving it. The centurion is not content to watch his friend lie paralyzed and in great pain while death wins. The officer knows and loves this man, and instead goes to the One who can make a difference. Expecting that the Messiah will do the right thing, he lays out his servant's situation.

Who in your life will do this for you? Where are the officers to intercede, intervene, place your case before the Most High King?

And for whom will you intercede? Whose names will pour from your lips as you bang on heaven's door, stating your loved ones'—or even your enemies'—problems and waiting for the Healer to come?

When on our own sickbed, our world shrinks to include only our own problems. But one benefit to paralysis is its slowing, forcing stillness upon us. Into that wordless gap, God has a chance to speak, and we are indeed slowed enough to hear and to listen.

Name your paralysis. Where has your illness rendered you self-centered and narrow? Or have you, instead, lived in denial of your problems and never caught up with yourself? Let your paralysis bring you to a place of stillness, and invite God to speak into that silence.

Wait there.

Listen to your own heartbeat. And while you're listening, ask the Lord to tune you into the heartbeat of those around you, to their pain and paralysis.

Just Forget It

Still, I woke up yesterday and decided to forget working on an area God has been relentlessly impressing on me, like some omnipresent sticky note always flying out of somewhere to land on my forehead.

Groaning, I plodded to the coffeepot, my mind set. *Just forget it. I'm tired of it. I quit.*

So the sticky note method changed forms. A scripture popped into my head: "He who began a good work in you will perfect it until the day of Christ Jesus" (Philippians 1:6).

Oh.

I may want to forget it, but God is not finished. And Jesus is the "perfecter of faith" (Hebrews 12:2).

God is always at work, tirelessly seeking to bring us to a place of perfection, gradually drawing us closer to completion. I am an unfinished project. Still a little paralysis hidden here, a tiny oozing bedsore there.

What is your soul's unfinished business? Your temperament? Your attitude? Are you prejudiced? mean, manipulative, sullen, touchy, controlling, whiny? Is there a pattern to your problems? We need some sort of paralysis probe, like a neurologist uses to test nerves to see which ones respond, so we can recognize where we're dying, where we have no feeling, where we've been unable to move in the days, weeks, months, years of our lives. Find a safe critique partner who, without anger or a hidden agenda, can mirror your targets for growth, places where partial paralysis hides.

A few months ago, Rich and I noticed a rowboat too near the shoreline for rowing or fishing. The men weren't fishing with poles but had some sort of stick. Playing crime patrol, we found they had a stun gun that zapped the bass. The hunters then netted the bass and dropped them into coolers. Dead.

Safety is paramount when examining your stun gunned places. Beware of those who will project their own brokenness and misery on you, wield their own stun gun, demanding that you "grow up" when they have no intention of doing so themselves. You may be a convenient fishing ground, so make sure you have a NO STUN GUNS ALLOWED boundary or sign.

Defects, Dysfunction, and Delight

The support group meetings invariably recited characteristics, standard "defects" in people of dysfunction. And one of the twelve steps calls for a "searching and fearless moral inventory." Take stock. You're a project.

But you're also a piece of work. A delight. God whistles when he sees you, in spite of your numbness, in spite of the stench of the bedsore from being unable to move or turn.

God is not limited by our paralysis. He is the Great Physician, not bound or bamboozled by our sleight of hand, our tricks of the trade to pretend fine-ness, our denial of our own incompletion.

It may take many surgeries of the soul, but God is not tired. What stops you, then, from being whole and holy?

Personally, being the one under the microscope wearies me. I want someone else under that little intense lens with me, or better yet, instead of me. And others' dysfunctions are easy to spot, glaring in obviousness, and surely more inconvenient and probably worse than mine.

Besides, I don't want to be forced into growth if others aren't also shoved under God's florescent grow light.

So I resort to the *Oh, grow up!* scream that only echoes on the insides of my brain. This is another mark of my immaturity, my half-baked, somewhat stunned soul.

But God waits, kind, a little sad, with an "I love you still" smile on his face. This is not about some neighbor's paralysis problem. It's about mine.

If I become who God created me to be, then I hope others will be attracted to the miracle of the healing, to the Surgeon who operated. Naturally, it's more comfortable if others lie on the operating table, if they need sutures or frontal lobe repair. And of course, they have their own secret sicknesses, their own need to take inventory, to schedule a checkup under the physician.

Perhaps you can help the Holy Spirit: "Hmm. Here's something that needs a teensy bit of help," you could suggest, while surveying the wreckage of a car they destroyed while driving under the influence, or the hole in the wall left by an angry fist. But it doesn't matter if no one around you gets well.

What about your paralysis? You don't get to drag them to the Surgeon and still try to delay or deflect or even defeat your own healing. This standard technique in retarding personal growth will not help you heal.

You will still be incapacitated.

The Servant

Imagine the servant, paralyzed and in great pain at home, likely dying. He is far removed from the Jesus clusters and crowds, from the *ooohing* and *ahhhing* and the miraculous.

Suddenly, unmistakably, into his private anguish and fear, the nerves in his body tingle. Feeling, glorious feeling, returns. The pain flees. His limbs twitch and tremble, and then he springs out of bed, throws off his sick clothes, grabs his day robe, runs outside.

"I'm healed! I can feel! I can move!" His shouts alert the other household members. Neighbors hurry to their doors. Their hearts leap with hope and possibility.

And with every step, for the rest of his life, does he remember the paralysis, the helplessness of immobility, and the surging new life? Does he live every day like a balloon blasted full of helium, bobbing about in exhilaration and unrestrainable joy?

I hope so.

Jesus Will Come

Savor Jesus's words: "I will come and heal him." Insert your name into the proper place. Hear the Savior: "I will come and heal you."

You.

Read that again slowly: "I will come and heal you."

Come for healing. It is the healing of years. Many years, many prayers, many tears. Come for healing. Jesus promised, answering even the unasked request, "I will come and heal him." If Jesus came for life—and he did—then that life looks like healing. How will you seek healing? Might your healing look like a rebuilding of your fraying heart, your damaged femininity, your view of others, your wounded child within? A healing of memories, taking you back to painful places that flash into your present like fire, leaving a wake of charred ruins?

How will you cooperate with the healing Christ comes to bring you? Will it be exercising forgiveness? visiting a doctor? accountability with addictions? a support group or counseling or mentoring or a wise listening partner?

It's never too late to become whole, never too late to receive the healing Jesus lives to offer. "I will come and heal you," Jesus says to us, as he said to the centurion about the servant.

Yes, Jesus will come. Put your hope before him, whatever that request entails. Spread your hands in a silent offering, a submitting of your soul and needs, relinquishing your unspoken but tremulous yearnings to him.

And then release it all: how healing looks, the heaviness of the pain, the agony of unanswered prayer. The loss, the disappointment, the dilapidated heart.

Let Jesus come, in his way. Let him define healing for you today.

Jesus came that you may have life, and have it abundantly. That includes healing your heart, healing your soul, making you whole.

So get going. The old stuff has been hanging around too long. Haul yourself into the Lord's presence. State your problem. See what he will do. And listen, one more time:

"I will come and heal you."

 • come and consider •

"I will come and heal you,"
He says, with a large smile on his bronzed face.
"But Lord…" I hem and haw, jiggle my foot in the sand,
"I'm not worthy. I don't deserve…"
The Savior interrupts, a gentle hand on my arm,
"But I came for life, and there is death still in you.
Death of dreams, dying hope, long-term pain."
He says it again, voice eager, joy radiating like
The sun,
"I will come and heal you."
I stop, and listen to my heart thudding. It bounces
Against my blouse.
And it hurts. I locate the pain, the loss;
I feel the sting of years of too much anger,
Of unforgiveness,
Of silence when I needed words,
Of words when I needed stillness.
The warranty expired;

It's time to let go
And get going.
So I open my hands
And my heart like tulips in the morning
After a cold night,
And smile.
"Come, Lord Jesus. I want to be healed."

• come for life •

Therefore we have been buried with Him through baptism into death, so that as Christ was raised from the dead through the glory of the Father, so we too might walk in newness of life.
Romans 6:4

• come closer •

- Locate your paralysis. Where does it originate? With what issues, events, people, wounds?
- In what areas do your loved ones hope you will grow? Ask for a little (safe) checkup. And can they identify where you have grown and changed? Do you see those places in yourself?
- How has paralysis created self-focus in you?
- Who invites you into healing, like the officer invited his servant? How well do you receive feedback about growing areas?
- For whom do you intercede, intervene?

• come home •

Father,
I have been paralyzed too long,

immobilized by fear,
by past pain,
by dead and dying hopes and dreams.

I invite you now to enter.
Show me where I am not caught up with myself.
Enter my paralysis.
Breathe life into my withered limbs.
Speak peace to my frayed nerves,
the scattered parts of my soul.
Come, Lord Jesus, and heal me.
Amen.

• come today •

How will you come today for healing?

come
for relief

"Come to Me, all who are weary and
heavy-laden, and I will give you rest."
—Matthew 11:28

. . . . .

Come unto Me, ye weary,
    Sorrowing ones oppressed;
    I am your tender Shepherd,
    Waiting to give you rest.
    Come, come, come unto Me,
    Weary and sore distressed;
    Come, come, come unto Me,
    Come unto Me and rest.
            FANNY CROSBY

From the bottom looking up, the incline seemed manageable. I
grabbed the watermelon, abandoned after a game of watermelon football, and dashed up the hill. I only walk if I'm holding
hands with my husband. For every run up that slope, I figure my

glutes will thank me. And my heart, if it survives the ascent. And maybe my husband too, if I run it often enough so that my rear end stops its downhill momentum.

But I'd never run up the hill with twenty-five pounds of dead weight before. Less than halfway into the climb, my heart kicked into panic mode, a bass drum threatening to thud through my sternum. Suddenly the watermelon weighed two hundred and fifty pounds; my arms felt like broom bristles, and my legs turned to poorly set jelly.

Some days are like that: plowing uphill hauling a watermelon of fear, sin, regrets, and other leftovers.

I'm not much fun on those days.

Heavy-Laden

Spiritually speaking, exhaustion is now politically correct. We talk a lot about rest, all the while ticking off on our mental fingers the lack of sleep and the gruesome work days, the numbers of committees and other commitments. Sleep deprivation warrants a badge of honor in some circles. However, this is larger than physical fatigue.

This week, a gentleman helped me heft my luggage aboard the commuter train, and I plopped into the only available seat for the ride home from O'Hare. When my suitcase shifted and nudged my neighbor's toe, I really looked at her while apologizing.

Deep shadows underscored weary eyes, magnified by her glasses. "Are you tired?" I asked. It wasn't a rhetorical question. I hoped she would answer, but her posture and her smudges spoke for her. She nodded, blinked slowly from the effort.

"Do you have a hard night ahead?"

"Last night my mother was diagnosed with leukemia in the emergency room." Her voice shredded at the word, and moisture seeped into the intricate webs beneath her eyes. She made no effort to wipe away the evidence of her anguish. "I never got along with her very well, but about four years ago we worked things out." Another exhale, heavy with pain. "I feel ripped off not to have more time with her."

Heavy-laden. Everyone is, and it reaches far deeper than tiredness or too much to do. With all the weights we carry about, we should be professional body builders competing in the Ms. Olympia contest. We feel it in burning shoulders, stiff necks, aching backs, breaking hearts, and thundering sighs. The weight wedges itself between us and our loved ones as we wonder, *How can I possibly give adequate love and care to these people right now? I haven't an ounce of emotional energy for them.* So we avert our gaze, pick up our packs, and keep trucking.

Stop Right There

Wait. Just wait one minute. Before you bend over and lug that backpack to your shoulders, listen for a second.

Listen to your body. What is it telling you about your weightlifting regime? What is your heart moaning as you brace yourself to resume the calisthenics? How is your gut protesting as you steel yourself to press on?

Long ago, an advertising campaign asked, "How do you spell relief?" The answer, of course, was an antacid tablet, something to coat all the toxicity of a lifestyle so that the lifestyle could continue. Don't coat the acid. Listen. Do you hear?

And then, listen again, to another voice, the voice of One who loves you, longs for you:

"Come to Me, all who are weary and heavy-laden, and I will give you rest. Take My yoke upon you and learn from Me, for I am gentle and humble in heart, and you will find rest for your souls. For My yoke is easy and My burden is light" (Matthew 11:28–30).

It's Jesus, inviting us to take stock and then to take flight—to flee our destructive weight-bearing workout and run to him.

When the Bottom Falls Out

Weeds choked our flowerbeds—not only innocuous little weeds, but the tall, thistly kind with sharp spines and deep roots. I toted out a brown paper lawn bag and began digging out the roots with a shovel, pitching them and their clinging dirt and spiraling top growth into the sack.

After affixing a waste sticker to the bag, both of which we had to pay for (that hurts my soul), the bag wasn't full. Rather than plop a half-full bag of weeds at the curb for pickup, I set it under the awning so I could finish filling it another time and get my money's worth out of both sticker and sack.

Yesterday I headed back to the yard carrying the lawn bag. Sixty minutes later, with the bag full and ripe with decomposing matter and the pungent smell of dirt, I grabbed the bag around the middle as if intending to dance a slow dance. But when I hefted the bag into my arms, the bottom ripped out in slow motion. All over my feet, the grass, and the flower bed, dirt and roots and weeds splattered.

I needed to change bags, to relocate all the refuse from the old torn one to a new, upright one, crisp and brown and whole.

Do you need to change bags too? To transfer your load of old weeds and ugly roots and thistles into a new receptacle? When has your sack of yard waste split open at the bottom, dumping now-seeding weeds over you and your newly cleared spaces?

Don't wait until the bottom falls out of your life, your anger receptacles, your weed bags. Don't store up your junk, your pressure, your anxiety, until it reaches such critical mass that "heavy-laden" doesn't begin to describe your pain.

Weighed Down

Name your junk. What fills your sack? Is it other people's expectations? Your own superhuman job description for yourself? Perfectionism?

Tami couldn't get her laundry finished because her rules for perfect laundry piled to the ceiling. All socks must be blisteringly white. Try that rule with five boys, all involved in sports. She needed to sort all the outgrown clothes, but rules applied there too: nice items versus not-so-nice ones went to different places, and all mending had to be done in order to give them away. With no laundry room storage, clean baskets parked in her bedroom until they could be emptied. But they couldn't be emptied because she needed to sort through her kids' closets and drawers to make room. And her children didn't help with their own baskets of either dirty or clean laundry, because good mothers always do all the laundry for their children, right?

Tami's perfectionism stopped her before she got started. The results spilled over into her entire house and crammed her heart with a spirit of defeat. It also created friction in her marriage and embarrassment for her when company visited.

We should do it all, do it well, do it without help. Where do these Good Girl Rules originate anyway?

Maybe they came straight from Jesus's day. "[The scribes and the Pharisees] tie up heavy burdens and lay them on men's shoulders" (Matthew 23:4).

Maybe it's not perfectionism for you. Maybe your burden is the need to have a constant output of service and doings, always involved, running things, helping out, your finger in every pie. Christ goes on to say, "They do all their deeds to be noticed by men" (verse 5). Though we may be unaware of our motives, winning others' approval and knowing they like us or need us keeps us working, keeps us doing, keeps us stretched far beyond our normal capacity.

What else fills your sack? The weight of fear, worry, regret, loss, anger, unforgiveness, bitterness?

But what do you gain by hauling around those weeds? An ulcer. Colitis. Migraines. Fear of intimacy. Loneliness and isolation. Unhappy children. A disgruntled spouse.

This is off-center living, like a top wobbling off its axis. When we rest in Jesus's love, in the relief he promises, in the life he gives us because of his death and life, we live in the center. Our approval rating is found only in God, and we can cease and desist with all the load bearing.

How long do you really want to schlep around like an ant walking upright with a loaf of bread on its head? The word for heavy in Christ's "Come to me" passage may mean "an *abundance* of weight"—exactly the opposite of Jesus's reason for coming.

How bad will the weight need to be before you and your bag fall apart?

Casting

My friend's life seemed to have exploded with issues during the months we'd been meeting for our semiregular prayer time. Hopefully she doesn't think that praying together made things worse for her. One day, as she ticked off the situations for prayer, heaviness hung in the air, like heat waves over a hot road, almost visible. And then, the scripture came to mind, "Therefore humble yourselves under the mighty hand of God, that He may exalt you at the proper time, casting all your anxiety on Him, because He cares for you" (1 Peter 5:6–7).

The Greek word for "cast" means to "throw, fling, or unload." Imagine with me, then, taking up a monstrous bowling ball, the heaviest one at the lanes, and being at the top of our hill. Now, think through your overwhelming list again. Superimpose all that pain, worry, shame, regret, and grief onto the dead weight of the ball.

Now, pitch it down the hill. Throw it. Dump it. Get rid of it. Feel the weight of that ball leave your arms. Feel the weight of your burdens leave your soul, your shoulders, your heart.

That's what Jesus invites us to do: unload our heavy-laden lives on his lap, and then watch him; live like he does. He lives lightly. He doesn't carry anything.

"Learn from me," he says. These are words a teacher might say, but the promises he makes are not those of a normal, everyday teacher. And what do we learn from Jesus? Absolute trust, even in the face of the worst the world can throw at him: ridicule, torture, abandonment, poverty, loneliness, temptation, death.

He lives in absolute confidence that God his Father will care for him, will carry him, will empower him, and see him through. And he shows us absolute love—love that will never stop. Love wrapped up in a Father who loved us so much that he sent his Son to love us in person. To show us how to live, really live, in the midst of a world that demands perfection and performance.

Through him, in our weight-bearing lives, we learn those "unforced rhythms of grace," as The Message phrases it—the heavenly help that is unmerited and free. Through Jesus, we recognize that all our carrying is killing us. And in his gentle care, in his humble kindness, he shows us how to live again.

The Cure for "Woe to You..."

In Matthew 11, Jesus has just finished lambasting several cities—not because their sins reach new heights, but because they don't repent even in the shining brilliance of his miracles. "Woe to you," our Savior says (verse 21). "Woe to you..."

Then, after Jesus beckons us to crawl out from under our loaded lives, he smacks into the Pharisees. Their religious police scanner nabs the disciples when they pluck grain on the Sabbath to ease their hunger. The grain picking conflicts with the Pharisees's list of thirty-nine types of work prohibited on the Sabbath.

Next stop, the synagogue, where Jesus heals the man with a with-ered hand, saying, "It is lawful to do good on the Sabbath" (Matthew 12.12).

One meaning of the word *burden* is "to overload with ceremony or spiritual anxiety." I picture Jesus as a Norwegian, thudding his fore-head on his hand in frustration at both the megasinners and the self-righteous and saying with a groan, "Oy veh! Vat don't chu understand?"

The religious people do it all right, bound up in their rules and legalities, their perfectionism and performing. Conversely, the sinners sin like crazy while the miracles blossom before their sin-dazed eyes. But neither audience comes to Jesus.

Both groups get it wrong. Jesus knows we will sin, though we will sin less and less the more we learn to rest in Christ. The course of our hearts and souls after sin concerns him. What will be different? Repentance is the beginning of deburdening a life—turning away from choices, actions, and thoughts that rupture relationships with God, others, or ourselves. In fact, one root word for "rest" means "reversal": turn around. In that U-turn, that change in direction from doing our own thing to acknowledging God as the Lord of our life, the source of our life, we find life. Hear those words, that offer, again:

> Are you tired? Worn out? Burned out on religion? Come to
> me. Get away with me and you'll recover your life. I'll show
> you how to take a real rest. Walk with me and work with
> me—watch how I do it. Learn the unforced rhythms of grace.
> I won't lay anything heavy or ill-fitting on you. Keep company
> with me and you'll learn to live freely and lightly. (Matthew
> 11:28–30, MSG)

Listen to that. "Recover your life. Real rest. Unforced rhythms of grace. Live freely and lightly."

Surely this is part of the package, the "I came that they may have life, and have it abundantly" gift all wrapped up in Jesus. Just hearing the words brings an *ahhh* from my soul.

How will you spell relief?

 • c o m e and c o n s i d e r •

Come to me.
Steal away with me,
Hide out and snuggle up.
You are safe with me.
I will watch over you,
Hold you,
Love you,
Protect you.
And give you rest.

Give it up.
Give it over.
Everything.
Whatever binds you, whatever stops you,
Whatever weights you haul around with you.
Pass me the ball and chain
And let me carry them for you
While you breathe deeply.

Lay down your load,
My sweet.
You were not meant to

Carry this alone.
Come to me.
Come.

• come for life •

It was for freedom that Christ set us free; therefore keep standing firm
and do not be subject again to a yoke of slavery.

Galatians 5:1

• come closer •

- Where are you heavy-laden? How does it show up in your
  body? your heart? your relationship with God, with yourself,
  with others?
- What is the root of your heaviness? When do you feel it the
  most?
- Which of the things in your sack are necessary to heft?
- Consider the bowling ball exercise: in your mind, name and
  transfer your weights to that ball. Invite Jesus to carry those
  weights, then heave the bowling ball away from you (prefer-
  ably not onto your hardwood floors).
- What will keep you from trusting Jesus, from believing his
  invitation to "Come to Me, all who are weary and heavy-
  laden"? What will you gain if you don't trust him? What
  will it cost you to carry the sack yourself?

• come home •

Father God,
I come to you

so weary,
heavy-laden;
bound by rules,
and wounded by pain,
and wrecked by sin.
I am worn out
with my watermelon-hauling,
weed-bag lifestyle.
The burden of perfectionism
breaks my back,
breaks my heart,
breaks my spirit,
breaks my relationships.
My bag overflows,
and the bottom is ripping,
and I long to set it down.
But I am afraid to let go,
and
I am afraid I am too weary,
too discouraged,
to even come to you.
Could you, please,
come to me?
Amen.

• come today •

How will you come today for relief?

come
when you're
lost

"For the Son of Man has come to seek
and to save that which was lost."
—Luke 19:10

· · · · ·

Come down, O love divine,
    seek Thou this soul of mine,
    And visit it with Thine own ardor glowing.
O Comforter, draw near,
    within my heart appear,
    And kindle it, Thy holy flame bestowing.
            BIANCO OF SIENA

Neither of us had maps. I am directionally dysfunctional when I fly into a city because I have no reference point. She is directionally dysfunctional, period. So after my dear friend Shirley picked me up at the airport and eased out of the parking garage, she pulled to the shoulder and punched a button on her dashboard. In seconds, a voice said, "Good morning, Ms. Mitchell. Thank you for calling OnStar. How may I help you today?"

Shirley might have no idea where she is, but OnStar always knows. We still get lost when we travel to and from ministry engagements, but OnStar never loses us. And we get found with the punch of a button.

Who doesn't need OnStar? Only people who don't get lost, I guess. But we get lost daily, and the world tells us we are losers, and our heart and hopes tell us we are lost. Even so, deep inside is the anticipation that someone will find us.

Thankfully, we always have a tracking device on us, because we are made in the image of God. Deep inside, though we might not even recognize it, our souls still bear the imprint of God's hand. Our God is a finding God, who, from the beginning of earthly time, set his compass to find us and his viewfinder on keeping us in sight.

Our family collects compilations of comic strips, from *FoxTrot* to *The Far Side* and many points in between. In one of my favorite comics by Lynn Johnston, *For Better or For Worse*, Michael tells his mother that surely he's old enough to walk to school without her holding his hand. Fearfully, she agrees. When he leaves the house, however, she also sneaks out, and though she keeps well hidden, she follows him every inch of the way. Her mother heart readies to do battle with anyone threatening her son. Sweating, she groans an exhausted sigh of relief when he arrives at school.

What a picture of our finders-keepers God. He finds us, tracks us, protects us, watches over us vigilantly. The psalmist says, "Surely goodness and lovingkindness will follow me all the days of my life" (Psalm 23:6), and this is a foretaste of our Savior, Jesus Christ.

How do we get lost, and how do we get found again? Our life—

our abundant living—depends on it. I love the way Jesus rises above the crowd of finders-seekers.

A Wee Little Man

He was so short that he got lost in a crowd, he was so rich that he got lost in his money, and he was so prominent in Jericho that he got lost in his superior position. But when Zaccheus heard about Jesus coming to town, his desperation to be found surfaced. Zaccheus pushed through the throngs, standing on tiptoe, hoping to see this miracle worker. But he couldn't see over the people's heads, and he couldn't shove and elbow his way through the tightly packed body of spectators.

So he ran ahead of the crowd and climbed into a sycamore tree, hanging on to a limb to see the Savior who would pass that way.

The Scripture tells us:

When Jesus came to the place, He looked up and said to him, "Zaccheus, hurry and come down, for today I must stay at your house."

And he hurried and came down and received Him gladly.

When [the crowds] saw it, they all began to grumble, saying, "He has gone to be the guest of a man who is a sinner." (Luke 19:5–7)

(They didn't realize, I guess, that if Jesus ever wanted to eat with anyone while on this earth, his dinner companions were entirely limited to the type who sin.)

You have to love what happens in Zaccheus's heart.

Zaccheus stopped and said to the Lord, "Behold, Lord, half of my possessions I will give to the poor, and if I have defrauded anyone of anything, I will give back four times as much." And Jesus said to him, "Today salvation has come to this house, because he, too, is a son of Abraham. For the Son of Man has come to seek and to save that which was lost." (verses 8–10)

This poor man, this lost man, this short man with his tarnished dreams who sold out his own people for riches, came down from his tree when the Savior came by. And the Savior came to his house and came with salvation and restoration. It's as simple as this: Christ overcame all of Zaccheus's shortcomings. And abundant life flowed out of Zaccheus's home and throughout the town.

What a remarkable sight. The people didn't understand that, before their eyes, they witnessed the miracle of salvation, a lost man found, and the repentance that comes from restoration. Immediately the tax collector wanted to make amends for his sin by giving people back what they had lost: their faith and 400 percent interest on the money he stole from them through usurious taxing.

Before Jesus found him, Zaccheus lined his own pockets with others' wealth. After restoration, Jesus's love lined Zaccheus's heart, and greed had no place to fester.

His life changed forever. Because Zaccheus dared to be found, to come down, salvation found him.

Getting Lost

We get lost all the time. There are many routes and many paths to lose our way. One of those is when others sin against us.

For years, Angie kept her childhood a secret. Not even her husband-to-be knew about the sexual abuse, nor how those wounds erupted in a need to secure physical love from any guy she ever dated. She had become a boomerang of dysfunction, wrapping her secrets and her shame into a tight, dangerous package. She never landed long, making certain that no one's love made contact with her. The sin against her turned her heart to marble, cold and unfeeling. She lost herself.

Though she found Jesus as her Savior when she was a child, she lost contact with him, just like she did with anyone who loved her. But Jesus found Angie again when she boomeranged into the man who would one day marry her, and through that man, Jesus wedged his way in to offer Angie love and freedom and began to melt her heart.

This finders-keepers God doesn't want us out of his sight. So when sin shows up on the radar and separates us from him, he sets to work. When Lucinda's clients claimed to own some of her work and refused to release their claim, Michelle's blood pressure climbed, and she nearly exploded with frustration. She said, "I had a screen saver that flashed random Bible verses. They always seemed to apply whenever I lost my temper and got ready to tell someone off. But the best one came when I was about to call and really tell those clients how I felt—I even had the phone in hand—and the screen saver said, 'Wait for the Lord! Be strong, take heart and wait for the Lord!'" God worked out the problem without Michelle's sinning in the middle of the others' sin against her.

If you feel lost—lost in your pain, forgotten in your troubles— one way to find yourself may be to rail at God. Too often, in my own life, I take out my anger on those around me—or people I meet in my daily rounds or someone I blame for not relieving my situation— when at the bottom of my soul I am furious with God. I've gotten lost by blaming others when my anger truly lies with God: How come you haven't taken care of us? Where have you been? Why aren't you finding me?

When we can locate the source of our pain, we begin to find ourselves. And when we find ourselves, we will always find God, because he promised to never leave us or forsake us. So wherever you are, God is as well.

Regardless of how dim your circumstances or how massive your discontent, God has not lost sight of you or left you alone. Refuse the temptation to lose yourself in your anger; instead, take it to God and let him deal with it.

Misdirected Expectations

As I followed this pattern, identifying my anger and taking it to God with both barrels, I began to realize how I'd damaged my relationships by expecting people to alleviate some suffering or some problem, hoping they would be my answer, provide my needs, rescue me. Find me.

When my husband and I recognized the Lord's voice calling to us to move into a new means of ministry, to leave the pastorate and its fellowship and begin a nonprofit ministry, we left behind our pension, health insurance, term life insurance, housing allowance, car. And, oh yes, our salary. Thankfully we had no idea how it would feel to be absolutely bereft of financial backing. Fear chewed at me nearly every second of the day. I craned my neck for people who might alleviate the fear. Perhaps someone at our new church could come on our support team. Or someone with more money than we had could contribute to the baseline income of our nonprofit. There should be someone who could take care of us, recognize our needs, and meet them.

Astoundingly, some people did. For all my whining, God still sent hands-on, skin-on help along the way:

Bill and Amy shared their van with us for at least a year; we huddled over schedules to work around my ultraheavy speaking calendar and still allow Rich to hit the trail with his ministry...

Our friends lent us their sound system for Rich to use at the worship services he led, allowing us to store it in our home and then they borrowed it from *us*...

The Post Office delivered an anonymous grocery gift card...

Someone stopped by with bags of coffee beans...

The list goes on as gifts appeared, time after time, at just the right time, just when we needed help or even just the boost of knowing those around us cared. People loved us in such amazing ways. But they didn't—couldn't—cover our needs in totality. And my fear didn't leave. It would have been so easy to get lost in resentment, in wrong focus. "Why isn't the church taking care of us? Don't they know how hard this is? What about our friends who have stable incomes? What about...?"

I looked to this world to care for us, to find us and rescue us— and in expecting people to meet my needs, I nearly tumbled off the radar. Bitterness could have gobbled me down in one bite, like our Husky inhaling a pan of leftover spaghetti.

Meanwhile, Jesus waited for me. He waited for me to be still long enough, to quit playing hide-and-seek-and-diversion, for me to stop and be still and wait in the same place for a while so that he could find me.

This is his heart's desire. Author and retreat leader Flora Slosson Wuellner says, "We are not seeking a reluctant God who is hiding. Our very longing to feel closer to God exists because God already loves us, longs for us, has reached us, and spoken to us."[1]

Other Ways We Get Lost

"You are created to experience your true life, your genuine identity, your deepest meaning, your fullest purpose, your ultimate value in an intimate, loving union with God at the core of your being," Robert

Mulholland wrote.[2] "The temptation to take over God's role in our life is the essence of the false self."

This began in Eden when Adam and Eve weren't content being under God's supervision; they wanted to *be* god. They got lost, back in Eden, and we have been lost ever since.

It's impossible to find ourselves without using Christ as our centering point. Any other point of reference changes the centrifugal pull and jerks us out of God's love and presence. When I try to find my meaning, my value, in my job or my husband's income or in my home or our car or in my children's behavior or their success or lack of it, I am in trouble. I have pulled away from my true home. I am trying to take over God's role. I am lost.

Last year, I drove six hours to a speaking engagement and arrived in time to meet the planning committee for dinner. When I realized they were not going to buy my meal, I passed on dinner and instead dropped $1.39 on some extremely bad coffee and sat with them, inviting them to share their stories. Inwardly, however, I worried with their oversight like you fiddle with a hangnail. *What were they thinking? Don't they know they should have offered to buy me dinner? Obviously they don't care.*

Search Me, O God

When I got back to my hotel room, everything seemed tacky: the room, the engagement, the people. I am embarrassed at how upset I got. I obsessed for hours, and when I could finally get a cell phone signal, I complained to my poor husband, who sleeps on the floor in churches when he does ministry. (He was very kind and did not highlight this, nor that, as Matthew 8:20 reminds us, "The foxes have holes and the birds of the air have nests, but the Son of Man has nowhere to lay His head," which I thought very polite of him.)

But Jesus reminded me. His relentless attention during the night was straight from Psalm 139:23–24: "Search me, O God, and know my heart; try me and know my anxious thoughts; and see if there be any hurtful way in me, and lead me in the everlasting way." He did. I couldn't sleep, couldn't concentrate, couldn't think. I tried to work on the endless pile of to-dos I haul with me, tried to read, tried to escape. All the while, I knew God had work to do, and he could do it through me the next day. Or not.

Before heading over to the church for the retreat in the morning, I knelt and begged God's forgiveness.

At the close of the retreat, we offered an opportunity for the women to get found, really found, by Jesus. Salvation came to that house, that day. Nearly 20 percent of the women indicated that they made a first-time commitment to the Lord at the invitation.

Loading the trunk, I heard my stomach growl because again I hadn't eaten (this time because of food allergies). I began to weep. I'd gotten so lost in my equation—*if I'm valuable, people will take care of my needs; if I'm not valuable, they won't*—that I nearly messed up my chance to be a part of God's plan to find many women that day. Of course, he would have sent someone else to them, but what joy to have been a small part of the process.

Any time our meaning comes from anything or anyone other than God, we've pulled up our stakes and packed our tents and left home. We've become runaways, lost from God. But he will find us and allow us to be part of the seeking and finding of others.

Getting Found

While God is seeking to get us back on the screen, know that we have an Enemy who does not want us to be found. This is the last thing he wants, because then God's will *will* be done.

Even so, our mighty God will find us. The Enemy will not win the hide-and-seek game. We help ourselves get found when we:

- change our focus, raising our eyes from our own self-focus to God, his goodness, and his love for us.
- seek God in prayer. "Then you will call upon Me and come and pray to Me, and I will listen to you. You will seek Me and find Me when you search for Me with all your heart," the Lord says in Jeremiah 29:12–13. Yesterday I prayed over my calendar. Our ministry heavily depends on income generated through speaking engagements, and I can either fret and stew, or pray and move on. I didn't have time to fret and stew, and so I prayed instead. Into my inbox came three queries about speaking, all of which fit into the gaping blanks. I thought, *This is grace—this is God's kindness.*
- love with God's power, even though we'd prefer to be lost and alone to self-focus some more.
- worship. Focusing on God changes our perspective. We recognize again his power over our lives, like the coffee beans showing up at my house just when I'd run out of coffee! We see his hand guiding us through our days—the miraculous phone call at exactly the right moment—and trust again his provisions for us in the future.

In Psalms 95–107, all but one of the psalms begins with praise or thanksgiving, a recitation of God's faithfulness. Of the thirteen chapters, only Psalm 102 opens with a plea: "Hear my prayer, O LORD! And let my cry for help come to You. Do not hide Your face from me." Just as with the psalmist, praise puts our problems in perspective: God is God—and I am not! What a relief. God is good; God will be exalted in both the heavens and the earth. If I'm one of the earth's inhabitants, then God will take care of me.

God finds us when we deliberately connect with others, moving out of our isolation and toward relationships that will nurture us. People who love God ground us, helping us recenter on God's love and the right next step.

God will find us. But we also must force ourselves to move with our hearts and actions and words into the daylight to be found, by him and by others.

Sardines

Our son is the host of the year, and he loves nothing more than inviting over groups of friends. He uses every inch of our hill and yard and groans when we establish times that limit the party to five hours. The best parties go well into the dark, so that whooping, hollering rounds of capture the flag and ghost in the graveyard can burn off the endless s'mores and soft drinks.

The last gathering ended with a 10 p.m. game of sardines, a sort of reverse hide-and-seek. Here, "it" hides while the others count, then peel off into the darkness after their counting limit expires. The goal: to find the first person who hid and snuggle in beside him. The two then wait breathlessly, not revealing their whereabouts, sweat pouring and hearts thudding from the running and the hiding.

Silently, others will stumble on the hiding place and cram in with the group like sardines. The game ends when the last person finds the group.

Isn't this like church is meant to be, like the kingdom of God is meant to be? The society of the lost, the hiding, finding God, finding each other, and creating community together. The game ends when the last lost person finds the hiding spot, the safe spot.

When everyone has a chance to be found, the kingdom comes.

• come and consider •

"Come out, come out,
Wherever you are!"
Jesus cups his hands to
His mouth, invites you into
Intimacy.
Be found by him,
Loved by him.
"I'm here! Right here!
Come and find me,"
He beckons with his heart,
His hands,
And welcomes you
Yet again,
Back into the game,
Back into his arms,
Back into life,
Real life,
Abundant life.

• come for life •

I acknowledged my sin to You, And my iniquity I did not hide; I said, "I will confess my transgressions to the LORD"; And You forgave the guilt of my sin. Therefore, let everyone who is godly pray to You in a time when You may be found; Surely in a flood of great waters they will not reach him. You are my hiding place; You preserve me from trouble; You surround me with songs of deliverance.

Psalm 32:5–7

• come closer •

- What's your greatest "getting lost while traveling" story?
- How did Christ first find you for salvation?
- What about getting lost in your personal, spiritual, or emotional life? In what ways do you get lost? How do you hope to be found, whether in healthy or unhealthy ways?
- When do you spin off-center, trying to take over God's role in your life? In others' lives?
- When has God found you, and what shape were you in? How do you let yourself be found?

• come home •

Dear Lord,
I bring my heart-pounding,
running-away self
to you.
Hide-and-seek is fun,
but getting lost is not,
and I have been lost.
Thank you that your arms
are always open,
always ready to receive me.
Show me where I have
gotten lost,
gotten off-track,
and find me
again.
And again.

Thank you for playing
finders, keepers
and holding on forever.
Amen.

• come today •

How will you come today to be found?

come
for adoption

"I will not leave you as orphans;
I will come to you."
—John 14:18

• • • • •

Come, holy Comforter,
    Thy sacred witness bear
    in this glad hour:
    Thou who almighty art,
    now rule in ev'ry heart,
    And ne'er from us depart,
    Spirit of pow'r.

ANONYMOUS

She is helpless and tiny for her age, her head flattened from lying on her back in a crib day after day. No one really knows her chronological age because of her malnourished state. A death sentence hangs over her lopsided skull, for a baby in that country carries an UNWELCOME sandwich board, and girl babies in particular.

But in America, a couple yearns for years for a child; the wife's womb empties itself month after month, and in the red rivers of bereavement God speaks to them about adoption. So they fill out reams of paperwork, have their personal lives investigated, their character questioned, their references checked. Then they wait. And wait some more.

When the phone rings, her heart leaps and her voice trembles at the caller's words: "We may have a baby for you."

Life turns upside down. The almost-parents fling themselves into preparation, washing walls, painting the baby's room, buying all the teensies for an infant: miniature T-shirts, diapers, midget booties, nightgowns with drawstrings that close the gown like a cocoon. Blankets and board books fill baskets, and a bright mobile hangs like a benevolent happy bird over the crib.

They love this child, this bundle of need, this bit of life that to others is disposable. Sight unseen, the baby becomes the target of prayers and the long-distance recipient of a wellspring of love and protection. From across the world, the couple lavishes love on her. When the details finalize, friends drive them to the airport, a viral excitement spreading through the car and then spreading through the rows of people on the airplane.

Papers are signed. Money changes hands. Her adoption is complete. The new parents adjust their will to include her; and she, with her soft skin the color of almonds, and her parents, with their European-beige complexion, become a family. They had not known how empty their arms felt until God filled them with this warm bundle of grace.

And their loving gives her life, guarantees her protection. The reality of the orphanage and her abandonment fades, replaced by the family about her, the comfort she receives.

She is an orphan no longer.

Jesus Will Come

Before the Feast of the Passover, Jesus knows that his hour is coming.[1] He came from God and is returning to God. He knows that even now, preparations are being made for his arrest. Evening sees the disciples sitting with Jesus, eating in a borrowed room. Christ tells them, "I go and prepare a place for you.... And you know the way where I am going" (see John 14:2–4).

Thomas sounds the alarm. "Lord, we do not know where You are going, how do we know the way?" The others probably exchange glances, puzzlement and fear bouncing from face to face.

"I am the way, and the truth, and the life; no one comes to the Father but through Me" (John 14:5–6).

This doesn't really answer their question. And this isn't what they expect: that he, their leader, will leave them so soon. What have they accomplished? How will they go on? What's to become of them? Why is Jesus leaving?

Their worries must rise up, a damp but invisible mist suspended over their meal: their Messiah is taking off for who knows where, abandoning them.

Though horrors await him, Jesus is totally present. He calms their fears, like he has calmed the storms in their lives since he entered three years ago. "I will not leave you as orphans; I will come to you" (verse 18).

The Amplified Bible reads, "I will not leave you as orphans— [comfortless, desolate, bereaved, forlorn, helpless]; I will come [back] to you."

Zero in on those words. When have you felt *comfortless? desolate? bereaved? forlorn?* How about *helpless?*

Maureen's desolation began with one miscarriage after another, and her feelings of abandonment seemed bottomless, like an unending underground labyrinth. Gwen redefined bereavement when her son died, and her soul keened relentlessly. Jenna watched as though straitjacketed when her husband walked out the door and into the arms of a waiting woman. Comfortless does not begin to describe the bed of tears in which these women slept night after night.

The promise for the disciples is the same promise Jesus extends to us: though in this world we may feel orphaned, Jesus will not leave us in our bereaved, helpless, hopeless state. He returned to his disciples after his resurrection, and he will come to us in the final day. But he also comes to us now, just like his followers then, in the form of the Holy Spirit.

Come, Holy Comforter

The other day while riding the city bus, we stopped outside the Catholic Charities building. A heavy woman climbed in, pulling a flimsy wire cart behind her. A few small plastic bags of groceries filled the bottom of her carrier. I was seated down the aisle from her, too far away to talk with her, but I could see her sad face. A tear slid down her cheek from her right eye. Just one long streak that did not dry, a tiny eternal river carving a line of grief.

I began to pray for this unknown woman with such sad eyes. My cross street came. Tugging the stop cord, I wove toward the front, twisting between a wheelchair and other passengers, dragging my ever-present luggage behind me. Just before I reached her, the woman heaved to her feet and pulled her carrier along. As she stepped down to the curb and turned for her cart, we lifted it together over the gap.

That she got off at my stop seemed to be a bit of an answer to prayer, but I felt as flimsy as her cart. I had no money and had given away the peanuts from my briefcase. The single apple in my suitcase didn't seem like it would compare with the Twinkie-type things peeking from the plastic bags. So I simply asked, "Are you having a hard day?"

The river below her right eye deepened. She nodded. I waited, parked near the bus stop with my gear, her with her red upright cart.

On a sob, she choked out, "My daughter left her three kids in Madison. I have them now, to give them a home, but I don't have any money, and she gets welfare but they send it to her place in Reno, and they won't help me. I don't know how I'm going to feed and raise them."

A boa constrictor squeezed my heart. I refused to give her Twinkie-words. "I don't live in this city," I said, "but I know of a church where you could get some help." I prayed, she nodded her head, and we caught a transfer bus to take her to her grandchildren. And I kept dragging my life-on-wheels, entrusting her to the Holy Spirit to comfort her and provide for her needs.

On Our Own

So many orphans—abandoned by the system, by their children, by their mothers and fathers, by people who are supposed to care but either don't know how or don't choose to.

We, too, are orphans, some literally, some emotionally and spiritually—orphaned by adults in our lives, wounded by people who are supposed to protect us. There is no way around this truth: relationships are like hugging cheesecloth bags filled with glass shards. Cuts are inevitable.

Unfortunately, the cuts many carry from imperfect childhoods or defective relationships prevent us from going gladly to our adoptive Daddy's arms, from sitting on his lap, sobbing on his shoulder, showing proudly our crayon drawings, and reveling in his pleasure in us.

Sometimes, too, I think we orphan ourselves. Over and over we resist intimacy and move away from our loved ones and from our Abba, as Jesus called his heavenly Father. As a confused teenager, I used to push away my own father's love, when I blamed him for some problem or situation or refused to forgive him.

Because of earthly disappointments, we decide we can't trust our heavenly Abba, who is ultimately the only one we can trust. And sometimes, when Abba doesn't work the way we think he should—when troubles come, when marriages break, when children leave their moorings, when jobs founder, when the dreams die—we shove him away. We refuse to believe what we know is true because it doesn't seem to be true at the moment: that God loves us and will always, always act in a way that is best for us. This is a rule he cannot violate.

Inevitable Orphans

We can't circumvent orphaning in our own life or the lives of those we love. With imperfect people as a part of the earth contract, pockets of abandonment will always exist in each of us. Rather than dwelling on the orphanage, however, look at all the ways God provides earthly replicas of his parenting, making up for the inevitable bereavements of your life. Abandonment then becomes a gift that pushes us to God.

My grandfather was a gruff man, shrunken several inches by the time I grew to an age to measure myself alongside him. I have seen him in photos, much taller, with a shy smile on his face that looked as though a laugh would follow. I don't remember him laughing much, and when he did he seemed almost surprised by the sound, like rusty water spurting from forgotten pipes. But in his road construction business, working with all that heavy equipment deafened him. Maybe he couldn't hear anything humorous by the time I noticed.

Dust from the construction sites coated his truck inside and out, and on rare occasions I got to ride with him. In the center of the front seat, a worn cigar box held mysteries and goodies: narrow bags of salty peanuts, Wrigley's chewing gum, and pens with ink stains on the barrels that bore his company's name. A walkie-talkie squawked from its holder below the dashboard, just over the hump on the floor. This fascinated me with its suggestions of communication from other places and Granddad's importance. Sometimes he would offer me a chocolate-covered mint patty in its shiny foil wrapper from the box. But if he didn't offer, I was not to ask.

He was not a demonstrative, come-sit-on-my-lap kind of grandpa, and when my own children stretched their toddler legs and ran toward loving, laughing grandparents, I mourned my own losses. Maybe I wanted a television grandfather, someone who played with the grand-kids and beamed at their achievements and came to grandparents' day (though I think that is an invention more recent than my childhood) and spoiled them with treats and laughed at their antics and listened to their long stories as aimless as a country road.

Realizing what I'd missed, I grieved. I was never too certain that he even loved me. He just liked for us kids to be quiet and not too rambunctious and, of course, responsible.

Reparenting for Orphans

After Granddad's death, just six weeks after Grandmom's, a man in his eighties keynoted a conference I attended. Life lined his face, but on him the wrinkles looked pleasant, natural. I observed him from a dis-tance, not needing to get close to him. But as I watched, the Holy Spirit began to comfort me about my own grandfather. I surveyed this man, with his smile, his infectious laugh. I stood back a distance as he counseled people one by one. I couldn't hear their interchanges, but I could see the transference of wisdom and compassion.

I remember thinking, with a long drawn-out "ohh," that this is what grandfathers do. This is how they are. And God began to heal that loss, a loss that, even as I write this, seems insignificant.

But my mourning was more global, and the relationship needle that hits on magnetized spots stopped on Granddad only briefly. The grief was over many imperfect people in my life and my own insecurities and inabilities to love with very much enthusiasm or joy.

Jesus, however, promised a "Comforter," one meaning for the Greek word for Holy Spirit. By watching others around me, by availing myself of relationships that seemed healthy and welcoming, he began to rock me, cuddle me, and nurture me until I felt I could run and play and be part of life again. A group of women became my close friends, with me as their youngest member. They created a protective alliance for me, offering wisdom, searching questions, and laughing love. If they recommended a book or movie, I knew without question that I would grow from it, or laugh through it, and find God in it.

During my college internship, a godly pastor and his wife adopted me. Their daughter Beth became my best friend, and I joined the life in their home, slept over, ate mountains of popcorn, and got to call them Mom and Dad Whiz. They showed me new dimensions in parenting, and when Rich proposed to me, one of the first people I called was Dad Whiz to see if he would officiate at our wedding. Looking back, I realize that this, too, is the Comforter coming to me, healing wounds I hadn't yet noticed.

When Jesus said, "I will not leave you as orphans; I will come to you," he meant it. How do you see this Comforter? In whose faces does his light shine, through whose attentiveness has he offered healing? Please don't overlook or minimize such reparenting by God.

Through the comforting presence of the Holy Spirit, Christ comes to us. He comforts us through the Scriptures (see Romans 15:4) and through other people (see Ephesians 6:22). We are no longer orphans abandoned by the world and those who are supposed to love us the most.

When we say yes to Christ's offer to come to us, we are responding to an open adoption. We know our birth family, the people who surround us during our sojourn this side of heaven. We determine to love them though they are imperfect, and we get to know our new Abba.

Even so, we are only responding to his offer. God is a seeking God. He always initiates adoption. The child in the orphanage did not seek out her adoptive parents; they sought her. God, like those parents, made all the preparations for adoption, paid the expenses through the death of Christ, assuring that we would be able to join his family.

As his pledge, he sends his Comforter to move us into healing places.

Full Circle

Those adoptive parents with their baby girl live their lives expending love and support and nourishment to this child of their heart. Their daughter's adoption gives her a name, and all the rights of their name, and provides her with an inheritance, with hope, and a future.

They long for their love to be returned, and when she first smiles in recognition, their hearts turn cartwheels. At her first words, they sweep her into their arms and dance about the room, a crazy four-legged, three-person waltz of glee. And when she first says, "I love you," though it sounds like, "wuh-woo," their hearts split open with joy.

Imagine God's joy when we first turn to him as our Daddy, our heavenly Papa who makes up for all the imperfections of our own family and friends, all the problems in our relationships with others in our grounded, earth-bound state.

Sometimes, to make pacts with one another, children prick their fingers and smear marks on a paper, signing in blood their allegiance: to one another, to their club, to secrecy. Jesus made a pact with us, between him and God, promising to come to us, to adopt us into his family. And he sealed the deal by signing it with his blood.

He shines with pleasure when we accept his invitation to join his family, to take on his name when we respond to his love and allow him to sign the adoption papers. And true to his Word, he comes to us, refusing to leave us as orphans. We can say with the psalmist, "For my father and my mother have forsaken me, but the LORD will take me up" (Psalm 27:10).

Our response to such love, such comfort, can only be humility. We did not deserve this love, could not orchestrate our adoption into God's heart. And in gratitude we come full circle. We return the love given us by loving our heavenly Daddy. By loving others with that same love.

Paul tells us:

> Blessed be the God and Father of our Lord Jesus Christ, the Father of mercies and God of all comfort, who comforts us in all our affliction so that we will be able to comfort those who are in any affliction with the comfort with which we ourselves are comforted by God. For just as the sufferings of Christ are ours in abundance, so also our comfort is abundant through Christ. (2 Corinthians 1:3–5)

Though we may have an abundance of sufferings, we also have the promise of abundant comfort—comfort that we receive, then pour out as a thank offering, a gift of gratitude, to others who suffer, who struggle with loss, for whom the orphanage is no stranger.

The Holy Spirit comes to them as well, through the comfort we offer. It may be just a bag of peanuts or a prayer, but I believe God transforms those peanuts, those prayers, into a love offering, a symbol of his comfort, his Comforter, in this world.

• come and consider •

Dear child,
You have been hurt.
Your wounds have not healed.
People have betrayed you, left you,
Laughed at you, disappointed you.
Orphaned you.
I can see the pain in your eyes,
Hear it behind your too-sharp laugh,
Detect it in your posture.
Your fear is natural in light of your scars.
But my love is different.
I love you with a love that will never orphan you.
Come, desolate one.
Come to me, and
Let me wrap you with my comfort.
Let me adopt you,
Love you,
Heal you.

• come for life •

So also we, while we were children, were held in bondage under the elemental things of the world. But when the fullness of the time came, God sent forth His Son, born of a woman, born under the Law, so that He might redeem those who were under the Law, that we might receive the adoption as sons. Because you are sons, God has sent forth the Spirit of His Son into our hearts, crying, "Abba! Father!"

Galatians 4:3–6

• come closer •

- Where do you feel orphaned? When in your past have you felt forlorn, abandoned, comfortless? How have you handled that, then and now?
- In what ways do you resist intimacy? Why? How do you orphan yourself?
- How do you see the Comforter? In whose faces does his light shine; in whose attentiveness has he offered healing? How is God reparenting you?
- When do you feel the direct comfort of the Holy Spirit? How does that show up?
- How will you move forward with love, knowing there will always be "orphan opportunities" this side of heaven? When have you comforted others with the comfort you have received?

• come home •

Heavenly Abba,
I confess my disappointments in people.
I have stiff-armed others, determined not to trust, to love,
to learn to laugh again.
I want to be your love.
I want to relinquish all my hurts.

I want to release my bad memories,
and choose today to stop orphaning myself
by pushing you away
and refusing to love others.
I receive your love,
your comfort,
your promise to come to me,
and by faith I know you have.
Because you said you would.
Thank you.
In the name of Jesus,
who sends the Comforter,
amen.

• come today •

How will you come today for adoption?

come
for help

"When the Helper comes...that
is the Spirit of truth who proceeds
from the Father."
—John 15:26

• • • • •

Dear Lord! and shall we ever live
  At this poor dying rate?
  Our love so faint, so cold to Thee,
  And Thine to us so great!
  Come, Holy Spirit, heavenly Dove,
  With all Thy quick'ning pow'rs,
  Come, shed abroad a Saviour's love,
  And that shall kindle ours.
          ISAAC WATTS

As a child, I entered Dr. Seuss's world with full enchantment, adoring Theodore Seuss Geisel's *The Cat in the Hat* and other books. Who doesn't identify with Sally and her brother, sitting at their window, watching the rainy world with dreary eyes, when the Cat arrives full of energy, insanity, and adventure? Oh, the messes they make, the fun they have, the "thinks they can think."

But then the children hear Mom heading toward the door. What disastrous timing! Her impending entrance ends the revelry. The children panic at the monstrous upheaval created by the Cat and his cronies. But the Cat doesn't abandon them to their mother's wrath. He calls forth his secret weapon: a ride-on machine that picks up, cleans up, sweeps up, straightens up.

When my husband and I first set up house, within days I longed for such a gift. How could I have forgotten to include it on the wedding wish list? Oh, for a helper! A secret weapon that cleans, puts everything away, straightens, and cooks. But the helper of my choice would also help me lip-sync the words to the perfect song, words of wisdom and comfort. I want to know how to speak the truth in love rather than in harshness. I want to live an empowered life, brimming full with Jesus's grace and compassion. "Help is coming," says Jesus. (Okay, maybe this Helper doesn't exactly parallel Dr. Seuss's machine.)

Perhaps you relate. The messes I make are too big for me to straighten, fix, erase—messes in relationships, messes in choices, messes with my mouth, messes with organization, messes in my past. But this Helper comes just in time, helping us live abundantly now, daily, always. Living the abundant life has everything to do with knowing and being filled by the abundant love of God, in spite of problems, perilous circumstances, and far from perfect relationships.

When the Helper Comes

While Jesus and his friends are in the borrowed room at the beginning of the Feast of the Passover, Jesus announces his coming departure. The disciples, as we saw in the last chapter, worry about Christ leaving them alone. Jesus promises a Comforter, which is probably somewhat comforting. But much life remains to be lived, and comfort is not their only concern.

Jesus has told them that he is the way, the truth, and the life. He is the resurrection and the life. He said, "I am the Light of the world; he who follows Me will not walk in the darkness, but will have the Light of life" (John 8:12). He continues to be all about life, and yet now Jesus pops out with this surprise in the middle of their lamb dinner. He's going away, and yes, of course he will come back.

How on earth, literally, will these straggly, disorganized, jostling disciples begin to live like their Master? If they have their wits about them, they shouldn't—they should be scared witless. Their leader is leaving. Leaving! And the religious leaders hate him and will hate them too. How will they survive?

The Messiah has the matter in hand. He knew that they would develop some sort of amnesia, forgetting the things he'd told them, so Jesus assures them that the Holy Spirit has many middle names, helps us in every conceivable way. He promised to not leave us as orphans, and the gift of his Spirit brings the assurance of his presence and his power and the ability to live like Christ.

Yes, Jesus has to go away. But his presence returns through the Helper, "that He may be with you forever" (John 14:16). In his fleshly body, Jesus was not omnipresent; he could not be with us all, everywhere. When he left heaven the first time and came to us, squeezing into a human body, he opted for finite. But after he rose from the dead and ascended into heaven, he sent back in his place the Holy Spirit, who lives in everyone who believes in Christ. Jesus said, "I will never desert you, nor will I ever forsake you" (Hebrews 13:5), and the Holy Spirit cinches the deal.

Through the power of the Holy Spirit, God uses failed, flawed, fallen people to effect change in this world. Never lose the wonder of being just that type of woman—a woman who has failed and been forgiven, though flawed is being repaired, though fallen and has been picked up, who knows that God is impacting others through her ordinary days.

The Helper enables this miracle through teaching, helping us in our weakness and pouring love into our hearts.

Teaching Us

"When I first opened the Bible, I didn't understand a word in there," Jeana says. "But that was before I invited Christ into my life. After that, when I opened the Scriptures, suddenly it made sense. It spoke to me. It was incredible." This is one of the roles of our Helper: to teach us. Jesus says, "The Counselor, the Holy Spirit, whom the Father will send in my name, will teach you all things and will remind you of everything I have said to you" (John 14:26, NIV). This Teacher will help us learn to know ourselves, learn to sense our own hearts, learn to listen. And if we can learn to be still, we will also hear his quiet conviction of sin.

When our children were small, I decided to take them to my in-laws' cabin on the Upper Peninsula of Michigan—without Rich or any other adults. This does not strike me now as particularly intelligent or remotely wise, and I can't imagine my logic, but I packed our gear and coolers of food and headed north with three children, all under the age of eight. On a trip from the cabin into the nearby town, the car started making a lopsided, bumping kind of noise. Not a flat tire, that much I could figure out.

A few days into the getaway, I called my dad, who has wisdom about such things. "Don't mess with it, Jane. You need to get it looked at by a mechanic. You do not want to risk a problem on the road with your children."

In my youthful ignorance (read: stupidity and willfulness), I decided not to heed his advice.

The next morning, I crept out of bed in mouselike imitation, starving for time alone. Two rooms, three children, and one adult have that effect. While the coffee perked, I perched at the kitchen table, shoving aside play food for the kids' country store, rocks from the river, a children's card game...and flopped open my Bible. Or rather, the fingers of God opened the Bible, because Romans 13:7–8 leaped out. I felt like Moses on the mountain watching God write the Ten Commandments on the stone, except that I wanted to cover my eyes.

"Render to all what is due them: tax to whom tax is due; custom to whom custom; fear to whom fear; honor to whom honor. Owe nothing to anyone except to love one another; for he who loves his neighbor has fulfilled the law."

In addition, my Old Testament reading turned out to be—big shock—"Honor your father and your mother." Hmm. I wondered where I wasn't honoring my dad, and thus not loving him?

I called the mechanic, loaded the children, and drove back to town. After a paternal man with jewel blue eyes looked underneath the car, he pulled me aside. "You don't-a vant to be drriving this car like theese." I'm a sucker for Norwegian accents, so I listened hard. "You haf a tire rod problem. But I can feex it. Good sing you deed not go back to Chicago already. You vould haf a wrreck on za rroad." He looked at the children. "Verry baad."

Later I phoned my dad and thanked him for his concern and for probably saving our lives. And I thanked God for his living Word, made alive through the Teacher, the Holy Spirit. His convicting work and supernatural power were just beginning to show up in my life. Some of us are just slow students. Thanks be to God that he never tires of teaching us.

Strength in Weakness

At sundown on Lake Michigan, sailboats jut above the horizon like stencils from a wallpaper border, tacked there by glue-happy kindergarteners first learning their shapes. One night we sat and watched all the boats move along under full sail because of the wind. One sailboat, though, slipped past the others like a skeleton ghost ship, its sails rolled down, living by engine and outrageously priced gasoline rather than the luscious breeze that blew.

I know nothing about sailing. My one experience on a sailboat made me dry mouthed with terror, wishing I'd created a last will and testament, and I haven't been remotely tempted to repeat the escapade. I could only think over and over, like the song that never ends, *I have a baby at home! I have a baby at home!*

That skeleton ship probably had good reasons for not sailing. But I identify with the ghost ship: often in life, I pull down the sails and turn on the engine to get through the days, the waves. Running on my own power rather than the wind of the Holy Spirit—and running into my own weakness and inability to live well.

Romans 8:26 tells us of another role of the Helper: "In the same way the Spirit also helps our weakness." Under the Holy Spirit's power, we can live in the truth of Edwin Hatch's famous hymn:

Breathe on me, breath of God,
Fill me with life anew,
That I may love what Thou dost love,
And do what Thou wouldst do.

Our Helper helps us fulfill Christ's commandment to love one another, to live in unity with each other, to be his witnesses in the world. The Holy Spirit gives us the power to live the life of Christ in this world, to be Christ to this world. Otherwise, we are like the

Pharisees, clinging to the Law, trying to be righteous by our perfection. The sheer impossibility of being like Christ on my own overwhelms me. My greatest abilities fall far short of God's holiness.

Helper of Hope and Healing

Last summer, a friend and I team-taught a writer's retreat in Comfort, Texas. The Haven River Inn, a bed-and-breakfast, presides regally above the Guadalupe River. We arrived a day early so that the Lord would have time to repair some of the damage done to our souls during the previous harried months. My spirit felt like someone whose hair had been permed a thousand times too often and was brittle and breaking and falling out by the skein.

We sat on the wraparound porch, luxuriating in the beauty surrounding us and the gourmet food on our plates. We breathed deeply in the peace. For a moment, at least. Only one other table on the porch contained people: two garrulous pastors and their fairly silent wives. I wanted to be annoyed at the boisterous intrusion to what could have been a serene moment. I wanted to dislike them in their loudness, to say something to my friend about their disturbing the peace we were trying to breathe. My smallness appalls me, and God will always highlight it for me.

Just then, one of the men began to sing, in a throaty preacher's voice, the words from the old hymn, "Day by Day, and with Each Passing Moment."[1] By verse two, I stopped being annoyed, and a soul-hushing began.

> Every day, the Lord Himself is near me
> With a special mercy for each hour;
> All my cares He fain would bear, and cheer me
> He whose name is Counselor and Power;
> The protection of His child and treasure

Is a charge that on Himself He laid
"As thy days, thy strength shall be in measure,"
This the pledge to me He made.

I could not swallow for several minutes. The air lodged some-where south of my throat. I looked at my friend. Tears slid down our faces from eyes too tired to weep, and the Holy Spirit began to comfort us, to reassure us of his special mercy, his strength, his power, his protection. We were his children, his treasures. "The love of God has been poured out within our hearts through the Holy Spirit who was given to us" (Romans 5:5).

Thomas á Kempis wrote, "If the Lord comes to us with even a little of His outpouring grace to strengthen, life courses through us and our spirits soar like eagles. If we have felt out of sorts, shaken, or unstable, a mere brush of His Spirit makes us firm and strong again. If we have been cold, nearly dead in soul, the flames of His passing will rekindle holy love within us."[2]

If only we would always listen. That should be a shortcut on the computer screen of our heart, taking us to holiness.

Shutting Down the Holy Spirit

It was a stupid fight, as fights go, but I picked it anyway.[3] I am not always aware of the Holy Spirit's voice, but that wintry morning, I heard him clearly—and he tried everything but gagging me to get my attention and try to reroute me. I refused.

I don't remember how the argument began, only that somehow midstream I got angry about winter-wet boots inside, and the hand towel from the bathroom appeared beneath my husband's desk to catch drips.

Even as I distanced myself, feeling unloved (because I equate getting my way with being loved), Christ-in-me tried to get me to retract my ugliness and ask for forgiveness—to reach out again and pursue relationship. I kept walking away. How many times did I thwart the Helper's insistent voice?

I lost track. But because I shut down God's prompting, it took days to repair my relationship with Rich. He is very quick to forgive me, but I am slow to repent, and the longer I take, the more damage I leave in my wake. Cardiologists will tell you that time is muscle: the more time that elapses between a heart attack and help, the more muscle dies. The same is true with us: the more time between sin and conviction in our heart, the more death we bring to our world.

What keeps us from heeding that voice?

I wish I had a glossy answer to write up in glossy magazines. But the bare-bones truth of it is, we want our own way. We want to sin more than we want to listen or love. Sure, maybe my problems with inferiority raised their heads in the boots-towel issue. Sure, I stepped outside of the centering needed to be like Jesus there.

But whatever you call it, I still sinned. The only way to stop sinning is to listen sooner and to keep being filled up with the Holy Spirit.

Help Is on the Way

When Josh was young, he accompanied me on my weekly rounds to our favorite low-cost grocery store. Because we rarely shop at the higher-priced grocery near our home, on one necessary trip there we wandered the aisles for a long time, wondering where certain items might be shelved. Finally, Josh had had enough of the "I wonder while I wander" theme song and said in frustration, "Mom, why can't we just ask for help?"

Oh. Good question. "Mostly because I haven't seen a single person in this enormous store who works here, Josh." Then I smiled. "Let's just ask, even though no one is around, okay?" So with soft voices, we walked the aisles saying, "Help. Help."

No surprise that no one actually appeared in the aisles to help us, though by then we were laughing and had found what we needed. But this illustrates how we can live daily filled with the power of the Holy Spirit. We just have to ask. If our refrain throughout our day is "Help," then we have every reason to receive that help and move into the Holy Spirit's enabling power. So a day might look like this:

- When your alarm blasts a reveille, you pray, "Help me to receive this day as a gift from you and to be a gift to others." (This could be prayed alongside the "Lord, help me get out of bed" prayer.)

- As the morning crush crashes into the kitchen in the form of children, you smile and pray, "Help! The chaos is too much. Please bring me your peace."

- On the commuter train, you say, "Help. Help me to smile and shine today."

- At your computer, you ask, "Help me to be your presence at work."

- During a difficult meeting, you invite, "Help! I want to sound like you. I need your wisdom."

- In an argument, when you want to blow, you say, "Help. Breathe in me, breath of God."

- During an awkward parenting moment, when your teenager seems like an escapee from the summer camp in *Holes,* you plead, "Help me to love now." Or maybe even, "Help me to listen below the words for the hidden message," which is the same as praying, "Help me to shut up." When we are busy being right, we are not loving. And that is a key characteristic of a Jesus follower: loving.

During Advent last year, the time when we celebrate and antici-pate the coming of Christ at Christmas, I waited at a stoplight across

from a nursing home. The signboard outside the home read, WRAP-
PING PRESENCE. HELP WANTED.

What a lovely, inviting image: being wrapped, enfolded, swad-
dled in another's love and attention. A perfect characteristic for a
worker in a nursing home. And how much more perfect for us? This
is a hallmark ministry of the Holy Spirit: to wrap us in his presence,
fill us with his help, that we might become just such a people, wrapping God's presence about others.

 • come and consider •

Dear One,
I am never leaving you.
I promised, and have sent you my assurance:
"Do not fear, for I am with you.
Do not look anxiously about you,
For I am your God.
I will strengthen you,
Surely I will help you,
Surely I will uphold you with my righteous right hand."
That strength, that help,
Comes from my Helper.
Please. Be still.
Breathe, slowly.
Invite him, Helper, Teacher, Advocate,
To fill you with my fullness,
My power,
My love.
Only then can you live this life
Abundantly.

• come for life •

But when the kindness of God our Savior and His love for mankind appeared, He saved us, not on the basis of deeds which we have done in righteousness, but according to His mercy, by the washing of regeneration and renewing by the Holy Spirit, whom He poured out upon us richly through Jesus Christ our Savior.

Titus 3:4–6

• come closer •

- What messes do you make with your mouth, your actions, your neglect?
- When has Scripture come alive for you, as though God highlighted it for your conviction and application? How did you respond?
- Describe a time when you knew the healing comfort of the Holy Spirit. What was happening then for you?
- What about a new ability to love from the Holy Spirit?
- When have you ignored the promptings of God through his Spirit within you, through others, or through Scripture? How did that work out? What about the "Help, help" approach to life?

• come home •

Father,
Come to me now.
I am weary.
Breathe your energy into me.

I am wordless.
Speak your truth to me.
I am directionless.
Guide me in the way I should go.
I am powerless.
Fill my sails with your breath.
Send your Comforter in my sorrow,
your Teacher in my forgetfulness,
your Convictor in my sin.
Help me to live this life
in Jesus's power.
Only then will I live
abundantly.
In our Savior's name,
I ask these things, and
breathe.
Amen.

• come today •

How will you come today for help?

PART 3
· · · · ·

breakfast
Food & Care
for the Soul

come
for acceptance

"Permit the children to come
to Me...for the kingdom of God
belongs to such as these."
—Mark 10:14

• • • • •

I need Thee every hour,
    most gracious Lord;
    No tender voice like Thine
    can peace afford.
    I need Thee, O I need Thee;
    Every hour I need Thee;
    O bless me now, my Savior,
    I come to Thee.
        ANNIE S. HAWKS

At ten years old, my body was stretched out and gangly, like taffy pulled a little too long. Clothes never fit right, and my feet slid around inside my shoes. But even though homely and horrifically insecure, I still loved to go to the beauty shop on Saturdays with my mom. She always bought me a bag of cheese popcorn, and I could eat until I turned orange from the food dye. I avoided all the mirrors and raced up and down the sidewalk outside the strip mall, sometimes with my cute little sister who was all dark hair and flashing brown eyes. We carried tiny change purses and shopped at the dime store a few doors down, returned and flipped magazine pages, and generally felt like princesses because our mom went to the beauty shop.

Allergies plagued me during those years. I blew my nose constantly. One very bad Saturday, I clutched my wad of tissues, sitting in the plastic seats with the tattered magazines and carpet the color of rotting oranges. My nose started bleeding. I wanted to bleed to death then and there. A nosebleed documented the truth: I was unacceptable. It was bad enough to be Third World thin with ugly flyaway hair the color of dirt in a drought. But a nosebleed equaled social pariah. It was nearly as tragic as vomiting in the hall at school, which I'd never done, but my friend did once. I decided not to be her friend after that. Obviously, now no one would be friends with me.

Not wanting to bother my mother, who sat happily under the alien-looking dryer in another room, I mopped myself up as best I could, swinging my legs as though my future hadn't been ruined and I would never have a boyfriend or get married.

Unfortunately this was the day for my own haircut. I climbed up in the spinning chair and the stylist pumped up the hydraulic seat, chatting with familiarity.

As she leaned the chair back to wash my hair, she eyed the crusty redness in my nostrils. "Uh-oh," she sang loudly. "Looks like someone has a bloody nose."

All chatter stopped. Scissors went mute. All occupants gawked at me with horror and pity, adding a general tsk-tsk under their breaths.

Only the people under the dryers missed the vibes and didn't look at my offending nose and dismal possibilities.

I wanted to shrink to Thumbkin-size, or Flat Stanley and slide under the back door. I didn't need anyone reminding me of how unacceptable I was, how much I didn't fit.

It doesn't really matter how big or small the incident or how big or small you are; you have felt unacceptable in your life. Jesus knows this and is indignant.

The Mothers' Hope

Wise people, political people, wealthy people line up to ask questions, some with honest longings for real answers, others trying to trick Christ with their cleverness. The disciples, of course, are often first in line with the questions, and in Mark 10:13–16 they serve as religious bouncers for the too-eager crowd. The people had just witnessed Jesus's answer to the wily Pharisees about divorce, and no doubt the disciples break a sweat at the intense scrutiny as well as the answer. Perhaps they are tired and feeling intolerant. Maybe they forgot their juice boxes.

Breaking through the ring of intellectuals and scoffers and religious masks, the women make their way to Jesus. Clutched in their arms are their hopes for the future: small, sweaty, bawling babies. I imagine that the mothers wear sour milk on their shoulders and their garments are wet from drool, from diaper spillover, from baby liquids in all forms. Their babies are too little to be separated from their mommas and have jounced along too long.

But the babies are more than along for the ride. They're the reason for the journey in the first place. After his last stop, word spread that this great man, this miracle worker, actually compared the coming kingdom to a child. There, his disciples had asked, "Who then is greatest in the kingdom of heaven?" Christ brought a child to the front, saying,

> Unless you are converted and become like children, you will not enter the kingdom of heaven. Whoever then humbles himself as this child, he is the greatest in the kingdom of heaven. And whoever receives one such child in My name receives Me; but whoever causes one of these little ones who believe in Me to stumble, it would be better for him to have a heavy millstone hung around his neck, and to be drowned in the depth of the sea. (Matthew 18:3–6)

So the women trundle through, full of love and fear and hope. Barely half the children in the poorer societies reach age twelve. If a wife outlives her husband, she has no means of support except from her grown children.

Mothers: they go without sleep, give up the best bites of food, sacrifice time and energy and other priorities to care for their babies. They sport *eau de* spit up and don't have time for their morning coffee stop. Tennis lessons? Dropped out when they passed under the bridal arch, or *huppah*. These women raise their children and die young of exhaustion and illness and plain old worn-out parts. They love their children with a passion and want good lives for them.

"And they were bringing children to Him so that He might touch them" (Mark 10:13).

I don't know if the moms really know what they are doing. Did they realize they have come upon the Savior of the world, the one who will set the captives free? Did they recognize in his attitude God's presence? Did they see in him the twinkle of the Father's eyes? Did they know they have burst through the Good Ol' Boys' Club and into the inner circle?

They really should have been quite embarrassed. They should have turned around and meekly left. Except that their babies, wailing and squirming, wanted something more than the mommas could offer.

Go Away

The disciples, charitable only to a certain level, rebuke the mothers.

I am furious at those men right now. Their mothers should have given them a time-out a few more times. Obviously, they either don't have wives and children, or they snore through the babies' wake-up calls in the long nights; they don't change diapers and don't feed the babies bottles of expressed milk. They don't clean up their spit up and don't sit up with them when their tummies hurt. They don't mop the fevered brows or rub their legs when they have growing pains. I doubt if they wash their wrappers either.

In their tunnel-vision state, the disciples rebuke the women. It's as though they are saying, "Look, Jesus is talking about important things here, like divorce and remarriage; he's done some pretty dramatic work, raising people from the dead and healing paralyzed men and casting out demons. You wouldn't understand. The brilliant legal counsel is here, challenging us, and you make us look pedestrian. What are you thinking, asking the future king to bless your messy babies and lay hands on them? Go away, now. Haul yourselves back to the nursery, and leave us important people alone. We have a political kingdom to establish."

These women have trudged to Jesus, babies on their hips and probably with children clutching their robes. They don't have super-strollers or bikes with baby trailers attached. They walk to see the Christ, desperate for their small loved ones.

They are rejected for their passion and their compassion. They are rebuked for their perseverance.

When has this happened to you? When were you not accepted, not honored, not valued? When have you acted out of passion, your heart swelling with certainty, until you know only one course of action? And when have you been humiliated or dishonored for your intention?

The Savior's Touch

I love Jesus—his savvy response. He misses nothing, absolutely nothing, going on around him, and that includes whatever is going on in your life, in your family, in your heart, and in your world. Listen to him handle the disciples:

> But when Jesus saw this, He was indignant and said to them, "Permit the children to come to Me; do not hinder them; for the kingdom of God belongs to such as these. Truly I say to you, whoever does not receive the kingdom of God like a child will not enter it at all." And He took them in His arms and began blessing them, laying His hands on them. (Mark 10:14–16)

These babies are more than an object lesson, like a film clip in Sunday's sermon to demonstrate a point visually. Jesus loves them, accepting their smells and wetness and uncleanliness. He holds them; he blesses them.

Babies are the most powerless of all humanity, and therefore carry the least value, especially if one is setting up a political earthly kingdom. But listen again: Jesus accepts them, loves them, cuddles them, blesses them.

Corrie ten Boom harbored Jews in her home during World War II and, subsequently, was sentenced to a concentration camp, where most of her family died. When one of my friends was a child, Corrie visited her home, and this sweet saint, this victim of brutality and veteran of grace, prayed over my friend, blessing her. To this day, she feels set apart for having been loved and blessed even briefly by such a godly woman.

Imagine, then, what it was like for these babies as they grew, to be reminded over and over: "Your life has been set apart by Jesus, the Messiah, the Savior of the world. He held you in his arms, defended you before people who devalued you, blessed you, invited you into all the goodness of God, all the beauty of heaven. Stay with him. He loves you—he went to the cross for you, rose from the dead for you." Their lives will never be the same; they have been touched by Jesus.

This Jesus loves us in spite of our infantlike ways; he accepts us in our own messy, drooling, spit-up states.

The Unacceptable

Jesus, our controversial Savior. He gathered all the socially inept, the outcast, the downtrodden about him: illiterate fishermen, hated tax collectors, prostitutes and drunkards, leprous and lame, street people and worriers, and adulterers and thieves. The religious hated him for this kind of loving. They hated him for being so alive.

Rachel is a professional makeup artist, and every week she goes to a strip club and applies makeup to the women before their shows. They have grown to trust her, with her gentle, gifted hands, her compassionate words, and her understanding of their deep wounds.

She knows the healing power of touch, the blessing of caring for another with kindness. As they soften and questions dribble from their lips, they realize that Rachel loves them because Jesus loves her.

Last weekend, Rachel and her husband flew to Los Angeles for a porn convention. She set up her makeup station in their hotel room, and another volunteer directed women to her. As Rachel deftly applied foundation and blush and eye shadow, the women's hearts opened and pain poured out. As she touched their prematurely aging faces, Jesus touched their hearts.

Alongside the XXX Church, Rachel and her husband handed out one thousand seven hundred pounds of The Message Bible with their covers stamped JESUS LOVES PORN STARS. As Rachel walked from the convention center, she saw people sprawled in the grass, deeply engrossed in the Scriptures.

Surprisingly (or not), other Bible publishers declined to support the project because they believed the cover defamed the Holy Bible.

But Jesus loves porn stars. I want to weep over this truth. It is the essence of the Scriptures, the boiled-down sweet truth of the gospel. The heart-stopping, lame-healing essence of everything Jesus was about. *Jesus loves porn stars.* This is for the playground castoffs and the science nerds and the sports rejects and the skinny and fat people and the tall and short people. Jesus loves the people who've aborted their children, and Jesus loves those who've had affairs, and Jesus loves your angry neighbor. He loves the people who cheat on their taxes and the people on welfare and the rich and the poor and the mediocre. And the babies, the powerless people of our society. And yes, the porn stars.

Jesus accepts them. He touches them, the outcasts—lepers, dead people, women on their menses—people at whom the legalists would shout out, "Unclean! Unclean!"

Others tell us, "not worthy."

We tell ourselves, "not worthy."

Jesus fends off the self-righteous and smiles.

Hear him?

"Come."

Unkind Touch

Not everyone touches our lives like Jesus. Perhaps you've been victimized by harsh, inappropriate touching. Physically, someone has damaged you, or you witnessed violence in your past or present. Maybe another's words clawed your heart. The wounds go deep and leave long-term pain.

Like the disciples pushing away the mothers with their babies, others have pushed you away, not accepted you, not loved you the way you needed to be loved, not cared enough to bring you to the Savior—to let him hold you and bless you.

And when people touch our lives in hurtful ways, believing that anyone wants to hold us and bless us stretches our imagination. We also transfer that unacceptance to God, projecting others' strict authoritarian tendencies, harsh treatment, or degrading behavior onto him.

On a particular retreat, my husband asked the group to simply be still in God's presence—to listen, to wait, to relax there. A man looked up, frustration scribbled on his face: "This is hard. I don't get it."

"That's okay. This takes time." Rich is the most patient and kind man I know. "How do you see God?"

The man, long into his retirement years, paused. "A disciplinarian, waiting to punish."

"What if you sit quietly and ask the Lord, 'Is it possible that I am your beloved?'" (See Mark 1:9–11.) "'Can you really be "well-pleased" with me?' And then wait until you begin to sense God's answer."

The lights rose in the man's heart. He had made God in the image of those who had hurt him, associating human failure with God rather than believing the truth. When he recognized that God called him "my beloved," he turned to God in a new way.

We cannot deny that others hurt us, and if we can tell them that they hurt us without our being hurtful in response, we will be on our way to healing. But like the women who fought their way to Jesus only to be rebuked by the disciples, we have to choose whom to believe: people who don't accept us, who rebuke us, or Jesus, who said, "Permit the children to come." Others will always be around to hinder us from coming to Jesus, but you can check out the truth or falsity of their methods.

Whether you confront the others or not, your internal prayer dialogue might run like this: *I'm sorry they believe that about me, but Lord, you say to me that you've loved me with an everlasting love. You tell me that I'm acceptable in your sight. I choose to believe you and give my pain to you over their imperfect love.*

I didn't like the way someone loved me recently and fought against God in prayer. "I'm angry and hurt, and this is stupid. And I feel worthless." All of my sicknesses leered, tumbling from my soul in a deformed parade: low self-esteem, hypersensitivity, unforgiveness, anger, resentment, and a long list of others' sins against me.

And gently, the words pressed into my heart, "Are you willing to be loved imperfectly on earth, Jane? I am loving you perfectly, but everyone else's love is a dim reflection of mine. Can you let me love you through them, though it might not look like you want?"

So I began to look through the sloppy love and relationships to God's perfect love, reproduced imperfectly through others.

Though the day-to-day living would be easier if people loved us perfectly, in the long run, what really matters is Jesus's touch, Jesus's words, Jesus's blessing.

"Permit the children to come."

Hindering

The disciples' actions spring from their own neediness, their own longing for appreciation. Many men want a battle to fight, a kingdom to establish, and these men are no exception. Perhaps their own past nips at their heels. Besides, letting babies into the inner sanctum, into that circle near Jesus, messes with their battle. The innocence, the neediness, the body smells all hit too closely to their own core needs. So they rebuke the mothers and their babies, and in the process disown their own legitimate hopes for acceptance.

Whoa. Too often I am like those pushy disciples with my hindering tendencies. I fear that daily I am a stumbling block to someone. I have a T-shirt that reads I AM A GODLY BUSINESSWOMAN.

My son, hanging out in the family room where I work, overheard some of those hindering words in a terse phone conversation. He turned to me when the conversation was over and asked, "What shirt are you wearing, Mom?"

Other times, I hang up the telephone, and he grins mischievously and strikes a silly thumbs-up pose, saying in a ventriloquist's voice, "Yes, I am a godly businesswoman."

I either have to quit wearing the shirt when I'm going to open my mouth, or I need to look at my shortcomings. I not only hinder others from coming to Jesus, I hinder myself when I dwell on pain or discouragement or another's impact on me.

Believe me, I've considered pitching the shirt. But my hindrance issues are tied up in my own unaccepted issues, and thankfully, God isn't quite finished with me. Not yet, not ever, this side of heaven. Still, I'm going to be careful where I wear that shirt.

Like the babies, powerlessness becomes our entrance ticket. "Whoever does not receive the kingdom of God like a child will not enter it at all" (Mark 10:15). Our absolute inability to run this life on our own is our strongest recommendation to Jesus, because he waits to be strong in our weakness.

Jesus is no baby-kissing politician. Jesus loves those babies, loves their mommas, loves the people he created—and he loves getting to love them.

When we, too, come to Jesus in all our spit-up states, just like babies, unable to change ourselves or make our hearts clean enough for God, Jesus's love transports us into a place of life, of freedom. It brings us into the kingdom of heaven, right here on earth.

Life. Abundantly. Right here, right now.

• come and consider •

As a child, you had
The wrong lunch box,
The wrong sandwich.
Your clothes looked wrong,
Your teeth were wrong.
Your mom wore the wrong glasses,
Your dad had the wrong job.
You lived in the wrong house
Or the wrong neighborhood.
You had the wrong family,
Your parents loved you wrong.

You were too quiet,
Too loud,
Too dumb,
Too smart,
Too slow, too shy,
Too plain, too boring,
Too different,
Too skinny, fat, short, or tall.

You were not sporty,
Not smart,

Not popular,
Not talented,
Not funny.

Now, as a woman,
You are still wrong.
You are still too much
Or not enough
In the world's eyes.

But look into Jesus's eyes.
What do you read there?
Do you see them shine with delight,
Laugh at your antics,
Glisten at your repentance,
Light up with love?

Can you hear him?
"You are my beloved.
I am tickled with you.
You are enough.
You are just right.
You are—because I love you.
So. Come."

• come for life •

A new commandment I give to you, that you love one another, even as I have loved you, that you also love one another. By this all men will know that you are My disciples, if you have love for one another.

John 13:34–35

• come closer •

- What was it like for you as a child? Where did you feel too much or not enough?
- Who or what prevents you from coming to Christ? What wounds do you bear from inappropriate touches or words from people who have not loved you well?
- Where do you feel unacceptable? Whose voice are you listening to?
- How do you hinder others from coming to Jesus?
- What will it look like for you to come to Christ like a child?

• come home •

Dear Father, loving Daddy,
Others have hindered me from coming
like a child.
In faith and because of Jesus's love and
acceptance, I forgive them for the
wounds incurred.
And I ask forgiveness for my own hindrances:
of myself, of others.
I choose to look in the eyes of your Son,
to see the love and acceptance
shining there,
and to fly onto his lap, lean
into his chest.
Oh, Jesus,
I come to you.
My wounds feel huge

from others' hurts.
Yet your hands gently hold me,
loving me,
blessing me,
accepting me.
Bring me into new life,
like a child,
into your kingdom
here on earth.
Help me to live in that blessing,
now.
To grow up knowing
that you have set me apart
to be loved, and to love.
In Jesus's name,
amen.

• come today •

How will you come today for acceptance?

come
for light

"...that those who come in
may see the light."
—Luke 11:33 (NIV)

· · · · ·

Come unto Me, when shadows darkly gather,
When the sad heart is weary and distressed;
Seeking for comfort from your heavenly Father,
Come unto Me, and I will give you rest.

CATHERINE H. ESLING

When the electricity fails, when the lights give way to night, darkness reigns. Flashbacks of looting from New Orleans haunt me, people smashing windows and beating down doors after Hurricane Katrina tore life apart. So great is the darkness that looters don't even wait for nightfall; they smash and grab in broad daylight. Too often, darkness rules in our society, in our personal lives.

Her marriage was disintegrating. Never great, their relationship's decline accelerated when her husband filled his eyes with pornography.

Darkness descended so thickly that he could no longer see his wife's goodness, her heart, her love, her pain. Their life together turned into a sham. He quit attending church. He gave in to aching childhood pain and abandonment issues by substituting false Internet images for his wife and family.

After twenty-five years of marriage, she named the darkness. First to a counselor, someone wise in dealing with pornography, who taught her how to speak to the causes of the darkness without shaming her husband's fragile soul. And then, the wife shone the light of honesty into the thick cloud of evil and pain in their home.

His eyes were full of darkness, and the darkness of death filled his soul and his life and his marriage. But the lights rose when he saw his own brokenness and how it damaged his wife. Slowly the blinds came down.

They struggle still. But light dawns when we acknowledge our darkness, what living in that darkness has cost us and those we love. When we invite the Light of the world to come, he illumines our soul's night. Even in the thickest dark, his light can shine. And he waits for us to come to that light.

A Story

One thing about Jesus—he draws crowds. And crowds never fail to live up to their name—crowding. Even when he speaks words of conviction, words about sin and darkness, people crowd around him, press in from all sides. He speaks with such power, such brightness, such truth, that even though his words are not always feel-good, warm and fuzzy, seeker-friendly words, people come. They come from all corners of the city and countryside to hear this man's words about sin and judgment, about repentance and right living, about darkness and light.

Such words are taboo today in many pulpits. "Don't tell people they might have darkness in them, or they might not come to church."

I beg to differ.

So did Jesus.

People come to church, people crowd around Jesus, because their darkness crowds them out. They long for light, they long for a snuffing-out of the darkness that blindfolds their soul. The night suffocates their hearts and shows up in their shambled lives. They want light. Without light they die, and the Light of the world comes to offer just that—light and the life that accompanies it.

So when Jesus launches a sermon on their "wicked generation" (Luke 11:29), the crowds listen. No one wanders off to the concession stand. They don't want to miss a word. And when he gets to the story, they crowd in even closer because his stories speak to their hearts, painting a picture of their souls, highlighting their needs and longings.

"No one," he says, "lights a lamp and puts it in a place where it will be hidden, or under a bowl" (Luke 11:33, NIV).

Imagine them nodding in agreement. Of course. Why waste precious oil and good fire to create light, only to hide the light away in the basement? Why cover it over with a basket or a pottery bowl? That would be dumb.

Rather, the host puts the lamp on a lamp stand, "that those who come in may see the light." Again, heads bob. Who wants to come into a dark house? The people wait for the next lines of the story.

"Your eye is the lamp of your body. When your eyes are good, your whole body also is full of light. But when they are bad, your body also is full of darkness. See to it, then, that the light within you is not darkness. Therefore, if your whole body is full of light, and no part of it dark, it will be completely lighted, as when the light of a lamp shines on you" (Luke 11:34–36, NIV).

Feet shuffle. What is Jesus saying? We want to come in; we want the light, but…sometimes the darkness is our friend. Sometimes we love the darkness; it provides a covering for our shadow side. How do we light the lamp? How do we hide the light? What does the Christ mean about those bowls?

Lighting the Lamp

An eye full of light begins by knowing the darkness within us. When my ugliness sickened me to the point of desperation, I named that ugliness, called it *sin.* I knew that no light, no good thing, dwelt in me.

Being a good girl wasn't doing it; cleaning up my life on my own didn't work. I couldn't do it. Anger and sadness filled me to the brim, and I took it out on others, lived it out in sinful choices. The darkness swelled to such depth that I cried out, in the only way I knew, to the God who could deliver me. I needed a Savior.

We cannot create light from our own resources. Neither could Thomas Edison. Only God creates light, and only Christ, who said, "I am the Light of the world; he who follows Me will not walk in the darkness, but will have the Light of life" (John 8:12), brings light into our windowless souls.

The world will tell us that we can generate our own light. And that is a lie. Only Christ offers light, real light, lifesaving light.

Melinda tried all kinds of new-age drills, dabbled in Eastern religions—practiced some occult, even.

Her doctor, my friend, examined her at an annual checkup, remembering well her patient's multiple problems. Then, leaning against the counter, she asked, "Melinda, why don't you just give your life to Christ? Just get it over with and invite him to be your Savior?"

Even modern medicine, with all its advances, can only go so far.

Melinda disappeared from sight for months. Her doctor worried about where she had gone and how she'd responded to the invitation to real salvation.

The next time Melinda appeared, years had dropped away from her face. Light replaced the darkness that once lined her eyes and shadowed her soul. She said, simply, "Thank you for believing that I was worth saving."

Through my friend, Melinda witnessed and received the eye-opening truth of the gospel: she is worth saving. I am worth saving. You are worth saving.

Christ can be our light! As Zechariah proclaimed, "…the rising sun will come to us from heaven to shine on those living in darkness and in the shadow of death, to guide our feet into the path of peace" (Luke 1:78–79, NIV). He longs to extinguish the darkness within us—but only at our invitation, only when we tell him our life-or-death need, only then will he extinguish those shadows. When we welcome him into our life, to come and pervade the night, to be our Light, Christ promises to light the lamp of our soul.

Hiding the Light

But even when the Light resides in our heart, at times our soul runs for cover, pulls down the blinds, goes into hiding like people living in a war zone. Sometimes this comes from outside attack.

In England during World War II, enemy planes roared overhead seeking easy prey. Light coming through windows was, literally, a dead giveaway. Wise people pulled the blackout blinds and stayed inside, limiting the use of light. If a city covered its lights, dropping bombs was pointless, so the enemy flew off to locate other targets.

The Enemy looks for light, wanting to attack that light with darkness. As people living in the light, we are targets of darkness. It's an age-old tactic.

If you feel like you are living in a dark place, come to the light. Ask God, the Father of Light, to fend off the Enemy's darkness. The dark cannot eliminate the Light of Christ. He proved that when he rose from the dead and vanquished forever the power of the night. Call on the name of Christ to do battle with the Prince of Darkness. He cannot stand under Jesus's name.

How do you know the difference between darkness that comes from sin and darkness that comes from the Enemy?

As a speaker, I end up in all sorts of enemy territory: places where evil has run rampant, where tragedy scars both hearts and landscapes, where relationship destruction occurs daily. Inevitably before I head off to the airport for one of these events, darkness falls all over me. It looks like depression or picking a silly fight with my husband or problems with extended family. Inexplicable exhaustion may rush over me like waves over a retaining wall.

While the conflicts may be very real, my reactions may be unreal, out of proportion. That's when I must look for the Enemy's hand. If God's power works through you, then Satan wants to stop that power, wants to dull that light, and will use the people you love. If he can create enough havoc, we switch our focus from the light God calls us to deliver, to the problems surrounding us.

Once, prior to speaking to a large group of women on the East Coast, dizziness overwhelmed me. I knew it wasn't allergies; I knew it wasn't altitude (I am tall, but not that tall). As I sat at the round table with two young mothers on either side, the world shifted and teetered and spun, blurring my vision.

I turned to my friends and explained. "This is spiritual oppression. Would you please pray for me?"

I have never seen women wield swords so quickly and so mightily. "Satan, in the name of Jesus we rebuke you. You have no power over us, no power over Jane. In Jesus's name we bind you and your evil spirits and cast you out." Thinking of these women, even now, brings tears to my eyes. They have small children, work hard at their home-based businesses, at their marriages, and in their church. But their youth belied their spiritual might. I couldn't have prayed those words with that conviction at their ages.

There is no name on heaven or earth more powerful than the name of Jesus. The Enemy fled. And the light came, bringing life. One woman said, "Today the Lord delivered me from forty years in the wilderness." Another: "God saved my life today." As I listened to their stories of brokenness, of entrapment in darkness, of heartbreak over choices, I watched their tears fall, watched the weights fall away from their shoulders, and watched Jesus, the Light of the world, come.

So take up the sword of Jesus's name when the darkness does not flee.

Low-Watt Living: Dimming the Lamp

But sin dims the light and sucks darkness into our hearts. If the bowl snuffing out your light is from sin, invite the Light to shine and show up the darkness in your heart. If you can sit still and wait for God, he will come with his searchlight. Today I asked Christ to reveal to me my darkness. And then I waited, listened. Sitting still, without hurling requests and directions at God, is unnatural for me. The word pressed on my soul was *negligence.* I knew exactly what he meant. Negligence in relationships. I had been delaying calling someone whose very life was tenuous, someone who had dwelt in the dark for a long time. Too long.

Confession is nothing without movement. Lois Evans, cofounder of The Urban Alternative and a tremendous woman of God, says, "Faith that does not act is a faith that is just an act."[1] So I picked up the phone and called. We're going for a walk tonight to see how bright, or how dimly, the light shines in her life.

Do either of us have time to walk?

No.

Can I afford to ignore that word from God, that spotlight on my soul darkness?

No—not if I want the light in me to be light and not darkness, as Jesus puts it. Not if I want others to come in and see the light.

When does darkness descend? What snuffs out the light of love? Any time we want to pull the blinds, we need to question ourselves and ask God for clarity. We crawl into our hiding places when the mud of sin splatters the lens of our heart. I take the fast route to darkness when I don't deal with anger or hurt quickly. Letting either linger too long means it goes one of two ways: it torques over to unforgiveness or it spins into shame. Either way, I end up under the bowl.

The bowl of unforgiveness is a real light snuffer. Anne Lamott says forgiveness is giving up all hope of having a perfect past. That could be a past as recent as this morning or as long ago as childhood. When I refuse to forgive, I bind the one who has hurt me, and I bind myself. Once I watched a calf scramble, which is a lasso contest. After a calf was released into the corral, a youngster raced out, twirling a rope to lasso the exuberant calf. Even when the child managed to loop the rope around the calf's neck, though, the calf refused to submit. It bucked and reared and kicked and snorted. But the relentless rope had its way, and eventually the calf capitulated, tied up and bound—until the cowchild (well, there are still cowboys and cowgirls; why not a more general "cowchild"?) relented and released the rope.

That's what my unforgiveness does to another, and that's what it does to my own heart. What a dark and binding place to be. Forgiveness, or unforgiveness, is a choice. To not forgive is to choose to suffocate the Light of Christ within me, rendering me unable to release that light for others. It also binds the other with the same darkness.

Shame is the other route, the second fork: that pervasive sense of not being good enough, of being a mistake. When I make a mistake, it is easy to sink into the sense that I am a mistake, that I always make mistakes. A subversive self-chastising runs through me like a low-level electric shock, so low I don't notice it until, again, I am still. Until I ask, "Wait, what is happening here? What occurred just now that I feel this way?"

Shame can be a vague uneasiness, like "something went wrong back there," but not glaring enough to stop us in our tracks. Sometimes it's a conversation in which I didn't feel cared for or attended to. Usually, in fact, that is the root of my shame reactions, and the shame I often dole out to others.

Don't live a low-watt life! Invite Christ to reveal unforgiveness, anger, and other sins that push him out of the center of your life. Invite him to clean the lens of your lamp and make you shine brightly once again.

A Well-Lighted Life

Jesus calls us to walk as children of light (see Ephesians 5:8). In what ways can we keep our lens clean, our hearts pure, our faith bright? How do we bring up the house lights when it comes to daily life?

Sometimes dark days hover over us, not because of sin in our lives or enemy attack, but because we live in a Humpty Dumpty world, circumstances leave shadows on our soul, and life is just plain hard. Praise releases the blackout blinds and sends them flapping up. Calvin Miller says, "At…moments of utter brokenness, our strength comes not in the cry of our own weak name.… When our souls are in extremis, we breathe the name of Jesus…he summons us to bless the dark times of our lives. It is these which summon the light."[2]

Darkness creates the condition necessary for light to shine—thank God for the darkness and scoot into the Light of Christ through praise.

Ask, in the midst of darkness, "How can I bless here? How can I love other people in spite of the hard place?" This severs the pull of self-focus and flings God's light like a disco ball into others' lives.

Be a blessing and see what that does to your nighttime. See what it does to your relationships. One night, a wee bit ticked at someone I love, I flounced around in some gratifying self-pity. This got boring after a while, and I noticed some mending that needed to be done for just this person. Pulling the thread in and out of the fabric, reattaching buttons, I noticed my anger abating and my love returning. I could then return to that relationship, apologize for my ugly reaction. Serving another forces us out of our introspection and into life.

The bottom line of living in the light is that we are changed. A plant that receives adequate sunlight grows. And so we, too, grow as a result of living in the light. We become more loving, more fun, less angry, more forgiving, less impatient. If we're not changing, something is wrong.

An abundant life with Christ becomes a light for others. This is the mark of transformation and spiritual discipline: that others are impacted by the life of Christ within us, changing us. The Light of the world illumines us and, in turn, illumines others through us. Then those who come can see the Light, receive the Light.

Come In and See the Light

A well-lighted life is irresistible to others. When we live "wide-eyed in wonder and belief" (see Luke 11:33–36, MSG), we place our lamp on a stand so that others may come in. Jesus wants us to live as light in this dark world, just as he lived as the Light of the world.

Maybe that will look like blessing those who curse you. Or like love, joy, peace, patience, kindness, goodness, faithfulness, gentleness, and self-control (see Galatians 5:22–23). Maybe it will look like "transparency," the root of the word *light* in Luke 11:36: your whole body will be lustrous, bright, transparent, nothing to hide. D. L. Moody was a nineteenth-century evangelist famous not just for his preaching but for his storytelling midsermon. He once said, "A holy life will produce the deepest impression. Lighthouses blow no horns. They only shine." Light invites others to come in, come see, come live.

Today, shadows created by sunlight poured through leafy branches into our family room, dappling my writing paper. It reminds me of Psalm 104:2: "He wraps himself in light as with a garment" (NIV).

I remember, "I am the Light of the world" and God is "the Father of lights, with whom there is no variation or shifting shadow" (James 1:17).

And I stand in the window and pray in the brilliant sun, so bright that I close my eyes and then my eyes dance behind their lids. I pray for light: in me, in Rich, our children, other loved ones name by name.

Be light in our darkness. Separate the dark shadows from the light and bring us to the Father. Remove our darkness. Extinguish it—snuff out the darkness and reveal your light. Take the dark of sin away. Crowd it out with your brilliance.

Shine, Jesus. Shine.

I reach for my sunglasses.

 • come and consider •

In the dead of night,
Jesus comes.
Those who have sat in darkness
Now see a great light.
"Take my light within you,"

He says.
"Let me light you from the inside out,
Let me help clean the lens of your lamp,
Trim the wick, touch you with my fire,
And set it on the stand.
You are beautiful to me,
And I love to be your
Light and your salvation."

• come for life •

This is the message we have heard from Him and announce to you, that God is Light, and in Him there is no darkness at all. If we say that we have fellowship with Him and yet walk in the darkness, we lie and do not practice the truth; but if we walk in the Light as He Himself is in the Light, we have fellowship with one another, and the blood of Jesus His Son cleanses us from all sin.

1 John 1:5–7

• come closer •

- Where are your dark spots, places where the light does not shine? When does unforgiveness or shame trap you there?
- How do you move from darkness into light? How hard is that for you? Why, sometimes, do you choose to stay in the dark?
- When have you experienced the Light of Christ coming into your dark prison, like Paul in Acts 12:7?
- What will it look like to live "wide-eyed in wonder and belief"?
- In what ways will living transparently change how you invest in relationships? How will your well-lighted life shine so that others might come in for light?

• come home •

Father of Light,
be the light of my life.
Come. Bring light into
the shadowed corners of my soul.
Your light gives life,
and I long for that now.
Illuminate my heart.
Show me my sin.
Cleanse the lens of my lamp.
I want to live a well-lighted life
that I might splatter
a kaleidoscope of light
into others' lives.
Set me on a lamp stand
that you, through me,
might give light to others.
So that they, too,
might come for light.
In Jesus's name,
amen.

• come today •

How will you come today for light?

c o m e
for a drink

"If any man is thirsty,
let him come to Me and drink!"
—John 7:37

• • • • •

Come Thou fount of every blessing,
Tune my heart to sing Thy grace;
Streams of mercy, never ceasing,
Call for songs of loudest praise.
ROBERT ROBINSON

Two rickety laundry racks bask on the back porch in full sun. One hundred degree weather enables my tightwad tendencies in one way only: clothes dry outside for free rather than tumbling in our gas dryer. Heat blasts into the house when I open the door and jerk the racks inside. I slam the door, then strip the spindles.

Yesterday's load was old rags. It's like folding roofing shingles when I pull the cloths off the rods. Perhaps they will work as sandpaper in their next application, or at least exfoliation if one doesn't use water. I stack them like planks of lumber.

The insides of the washing machine are cool, filled with damp, pliable bath towels. I relish their soft wetness and the contrast with the boards I just removed. Before long, their moisture will evaporate, and they will convert to stiff rectangles of fabric in the baker's oven of the Midwest.

On Monday I got to help our daughter move into a new apartment. Signs along the interstate blinked neon warnings: HEAT ALERT! DRINK WATER! STAY INSIDE! CHECK ON YOUR ELDERLY FRIENDS! Sheets of rain had drenched every other move she'd made, so this was similar, except that the rain was internal and poured out of us. My clothes were wet from the inside out. Sweat rolled into my eyes, burning like battery acid. I remembered one reason I don't jog or do other high heart rate exercise: I loathe sweating. Sweating is painful. And messy. When I headed home after twelve hours of hauling belongings up and down multiple flights of stairs, out to the car and back in, lugging and tugging and pushing and shoving, the radio mentioned the heat index had dropped to 103 degrees. Well, that was a relief.

But water? We forgot to drink much water as we wrestled and pushed and pulled and packed. My legs started cramping, I got lightheaded, my eyeballs jumped all night long while I tried to sleep the exhausted sleep of righteousness. The next day, I felt like laundry that's been bashed against rocks to get washed. My body was so thirsty; only after a pitcher of Gatorade could I do more than wander around, lean on furniture, and fall wherever I landed, instead of doing real work like real people do.

Physical Thirst

In *Between a Rock and a Hard Place*, Aron Ralston chronicles his days stuck in a remote area of the Utah desert with one arm trapped between a boulder and two rock walls. Because no one knew his whereabouts, hope of rescue evaporated. He wrote, "For all the physical signs of my body's dire need for hydration, nothing, nothing compares to the anguish of my thirst: unslakable...unquenchable... unsatisfiable...insuppressible...inextinguishable. I find myself wishing to get this all over with to bring relief to the thirst."[1]

Water is an indispensable life substance. With it, our brain and other organs function, foods digest, our skin plumps up, our joints move smoothly, our blood is healthy, our body secretes and excretes as intended. All systems are "go" with adequate liquid. Imagine the difference between a grape and a raisin, a plum and a prune. Without water, we die. I have never known thirst and dehydration to the point of near death, but Ralston knows:

> Death by dehydration is turning out to be even more psychologically grueling than I was anticipating.... Waterlessness stalks me, the indomitable leviathan of the desert drawing in closer every hour. Enforced insomnia compounds my body's anguish, loosing a fourth-dimensional aberration in my head. I no longer exist in a normal space-time continuum. Minute by minute, my sleep deprivation dismantles yet another brain function.[2]

Given the necessity of water, Jesus's invitation in John 7 heightens my soul's awareness.

Living Water

October, two thousand or so years ago. For a week, the Hebrew people have lived in lean-tos, booths built to remind them of their deliverance from the bondage of Pharaoh in Egypt. Booths to help them remember camping, day after day, in the desert between Egypt and the Promised Land. Booths to remind them of all God has done for them, day after day, since that time, providing for their needs, loving them, walking among them.

The Feast of Tabernacles was a mandatory celebration for Jews (see Leviticus 23:34–44). After the people gather in all their crops, they rejoice over the Lord's provision for yet another year. This year, rippling like a brook beneath the songs and worship, people murmur to one another, one subject primary on their minds and tongues: *Jesus.*

He arrives in the middle of the feast and begins teaching in the temple.

"Whoa," the people mutter, "isn't this the one they're trying to kill? Where did he come from? Is he demon-possessed? Why aren't they arresting him? But wait—maybe he has something to say. After all, listen to him. He doesn't even have any formal education. And besides, they say that when Messiah comes, he'll do lots of great stuff—surely not more than this man, right?" (See John 7:20–32.)

Jesus's midfeast appearance is remarkable, and not just because the authorities wanted to kill him. In the middle of their booths, their tent-dwelling, comes the One about whom John said, "And the Word became flesh, and dwelt [literally, "tabernacled," or tent-camped] among us" (John 1:14). Jesus tabernacles here, sets up a temporary place here on earth when he moves here from heaven.

Daily throughout the feast, people sing and cheer and recite the Hallel, Psalms 113–118, which ends with a cry for speedy salvation through the coming messiah. "O LORD, do save, we beseech You;… Blessed is the one who comes in the name of the LORD" (Psalm 118:25–26). A procession of priests carries water from the pool of Siloam to the temple, pouring it at the base of the altar. This cere-mony commemorates God's provision of water from the rock for the Israelites' hiatus in the desert after the exodus from Egypt. Imagine

how many buckets of water it took to hydrate and wash so many people, to water the animals, clean the dishes. That God provided such
vast amounts of water, daily, for forty hot, dry, thirsty years, makes my
head swim.

How extraordinary that during a feast recalling God's provision
for thirst and while the Jews recited scriptures begging God for a savior, Jesus stands and cries out, "If any man is thirsty, let him come to
Me and drink! He who believes in Me as the Scripture said, From his
innermost being shall flow springs and rivers of living water" (John
7:37–38, AMP).[3]

That word: cries. Christ doesn't just pull on people's sleeves and
say calmly and quietly, "I have this plan…" like some covert whisper
in church, or like a spy avoiding arrest. No, in the center of all the
hubbub and pomp and circumstance, the revelry and festivities, Jesus
shouted. Shouted! Psalm 29:5 says God's voice breaks cedars. This
voice saws through the milling mob.

The Undercurrents

While in their desert transition, the Hebrew people subsisted entirely
on trust—trusting that God would provide for their thirst day in and
day out. Isaiah says, "They did not thirst when He led them through
the deserts. He made the water flow out of the rock for them; He split
the rock and the water gushed forth" (Isaiah 48:21).

In contrast, crowds who trust in the Law, trust in their rules, trust
in the obvious—these people now surround Jesus. Their experience of
a God who breaks open rocks so water streams out is the stuff of story,
many generations removed. They were celebrating a memory more
than a reality.

Jesus appears into the center of this celebration. "If you thirst,
come to me." He comes as the water, the living water. He enters as

the rock of our salvation, the cornerstone of our faith. Messiah is the living fulfillment of the Feast of Tabernacles.

If You Only Knew: Jesus and Thirst

This is not Jesus's first mention of water. Nor does he speak idly about thirst. He could just be talking theory, since he lives in total reliance upon God, like some direct hose hookup. But his earthly ministry opens with baptism in the Jordan River, and then God hustles him straight out into the desert for forty days.

I bet he got thirsty there.

And when, in his travels, he met a woman at the well in Samaria, he understood thirst when he asked her, "Will you give me a drink?" (John 4:7, NIV).

Her surprised response covered her shame: her history of broken marriages, her current living situation with an unmarried man, and the tiny fact that she was a woman. Decent men didn't talk with women in public, and certainly not with women of her reputation. Since even the other women wouldn't speak with her, she'd headed to the well at midday to avoid their reproach.

But Jesus knew all this, and he also knew thirst: physical thirst, and how spiritual thirst manifested itself in people who were severed from their hearts and their God. And so he redirected her questions with, "Everyone who drinks this water will be thirsty again, but whoever drinks the water I give him will never thirst. Indeed, the water I give him will become in him a spring of water welling up to eternal life" (John 4:13–14, NIV).

There it is again: spring of water, living water, thirst, thirst, thirst. Clearly, Jesus is up to something.

Fast forward from this well in Samaria to the darkest day in history—not Black Tuesday, October 29, 1929, when the stock market crashed and threw the world into the Great Depression—but the day the world crashed, and it appeared that God's plan had shattered.

Jesus, after brutal torture, savage beatings, and nails hammered through his flesh to pin him on a cross, said, "I am thirsty" (John 19:28).

Twice, soldiers filled a sponge with vinegar and held it to his mouth (see Matthew 27:34, 48).

The day collapsed and darkness tented the land; from the pit of his soul, Jesus cried out, "My God, My God, why have You forsaken Me?" (Matthew 27:46).

Thirst is sacred, a God given, God-seeking longing; we thirst for God's presence. "Blessed are those who...thirst for righteousness, for they shall be satisfied" (Matthew 5:6). Our deepest thirst, our greatest longing, is for reconnection with God, for that original relationship that began in Eden and was ripped apart in Eden.

When you sit very still, where does your thirst originate?

Not a Drop to Drink

Thirst is a powerful reality. Perversion follows fast on the heels of honest need. America capitalizes on this basic human reaction to dehydration. What did we drink before water came in a thousand varieties of bottles and price ranges and even flavors? Then again, how's this for a mission statement for Coca-Cola: "To refresh the world...in body, mind and spirit." What about the slogan, OBEY YOUR THIRST? or this billboard: IT'S ALL ABOUT THE BEER?

Is it really?

How closely related is our consumer thirst to our spiritual thirst? Jesus, keen connoisseur of humanity, understood the physicality of genuine thirst—and, like so many other physicalities, that it mirrors a spiritual truth or condition. Because both thirsts create such a commanding force within us, they are easily misdirected, misunderstood, and misused.

On trips when I was a child, one parent or another would sing-song:

"Water, water everywhere,

And not a drop to drink."

Perhaps this is true of our saturated market today. When the echoes of soul thirst begin to impact our system, we mask our thirst with parties, celebrations, shopping, eating, and other addictive behavior. Just as the Enemy tempted Jesus in the desert, seeking to lure him into trading in legitimate soul thirst for fame or power or bread, so he tempts us. Come, drink this, buy that, get involved in that loser relationship, read this book—listen to the perversion of the true longing that comes from our Creator. When we listen, we fossilize our heart.

But wait—imagine this! Jesus comes into the center of our rock-hard hearts, our stone-dead expectations, into the quarry of our desperation, and cries out, "Let me bring water out of that rock, those dead stones. Let me quench that deadly thirst; let me be your very Source of life."

We will never find life, abundant life, in the waters of this world. We might as well lap from mud puddles. Life won't show up from the kitchen faucet no matter how trendy that faucet's design. Nor from the beer on the billboard, the foray into sleazy novels. Not from the religious celebrations, from the rules and regulations.

When we look anywhere besides Christ for a thirst-quenching draft, we look in the wrong place. Like Elijah, who pressed his ear to the ground to listen for the coming rain, we obey our thirst by putting our ear to our heart to hear the true thirst, the longing that can never be satisfied by anything other than the living water.

Drinking It In: Slaking Your Thirst

The people who listened, who heard Jesus cry out at the feast, were commoners mingled with strict religiosos. And some people, of course, just liked a party. Roll out the keg, throw the confetti. But their hearts were dead because they had put their hope in what could never hydrate, let alone rehydrate, them.

I recently returned from an engagement in the Texas Hill Country. The guys hauled my luggage into the house, and I headed for the kitchen. I love them to distraction, but countertops are not their top concern. The sponge for the counters felt like a pumice stone.

Is that a sketch of your heart? When was the last time you felt hydrated, fully alive, a sponge spilling out when the squeeze is on? I want to be so filled with that living water that when stress clamps me in its fist, when my insides want to roil at another in anger, when troubles come, that love gushes over me and those around me.

But this does not happen automatically. This is where we get to partner with Jesus. This is where we hook up the hose. We propel our soul to the spigot.

We can't afford to delay the trips to the spigot, to head to the well. Some say that by the time we actually feel thirsty, dehydration has already begun. Not only must we consider how to allay our thirsty heart, we must also think about how to keep our soul hydrated before our soul is compromised by thirst. What will it take? To neglect thirst damages our own heart and relationships as well. When I haven't noticed my soul's longings, when I've run in the desert too long without visiting the living water, I take it out on my family. In my soul dehydration, I snap, bark, alienate, pout. Very attractive, isn't it? Makes Jesus look good. Uh-huh. Enhances my reputation. Right.

How much better to notice midrun, sip often, and sometimes

drink long. In her run to the spigot, Lynn takes herself on an "artist's date"—she gets away by herself to a place of beauty and lets God's nourishment soak into parched spaces as the heavens declare his glory. Judy straps her camera around her neck and sees life through Jesus's eyes, framing the evidence of a world spoken into existence by God. I love to take an afternoon or an overnight and spread out my favorite books, journal, and Bible while imbibing written words in a relaxed setting. For Becky, nothing but silence satisfies that appetite for eternity, and she breathes deeply while adoring God without words. Rikki goes for a long walk, praying aloud, listening for the Lord's soft response in the shushing sound of leaves in the breeze, the birdsong, the intricacies of the flowers.

Like drinking electrolyte-balanced liquids for physical dehydration, journaling, drinking in Scripture, or resting in God's presence restores our intricate spiritual balance.

God settled the dust in my soul with sprinkling rain when I visited a perfume counter and simply sniffed the various scents, pausing to really enjoy the luxury. Once in Chicago, I happened into a famous department store. There, designers had created live gardens in honor of Claude Monet, and above every counter grew thousands of bulbs bursting with colors, greenery and scenery reminiscent of Monet's paintings, flowers so glorious my heart pounded. I nearly wept as a long drought ended in that unlikely place.

But worship—worship is where God ultimately revives me with great gulps of living water. In worship, all my fears, my angst, my pain, my thirst are stripped bare, like bark peeled from a tree in a storm. There I realize that all along—my yearning as I encountered a race too long to run, a list too long to accomplish; as I harbored negatives from too long days in the desert—all along my thirst was for Christ. Worship whisks me to that fountainhead.

Please, stop where you are.

Sense the dryness of your mouth.

Notice how your tongue cleaves to the roof above it.

Hear the arrhythmias of your heart from dehydration.

Visualize yourself, like Aron Ralston in the Utah desert, hovering near death from spiritual dehydration.

And then, listen:

"The last mouthful of my water supply has become a sacred element. In effect, the liquid has transubstantiated from something of this earth to something holy and eternal—it has become time itself, and in time, it has become life. The longer that water lasts, the longer I will last."[4]

There is water, water in abundance, a sacred water that will last through eternity, an endless source of life. A stream of living water awaits you. Hold out your cup.

May that trickle become a Niagara of hope, of life overflowing, filling you, squeezing from you in the Vise-Grip of your day, laughing water that rises to your ankles. Run, then! Run, splash, play in that living water, like a child finally released from the hot, windowless schoolroom and sent out to the beach for the day. Race along the shoreline, dance in and out of the lapping waves. Know the thirst-quenching love of Jesus, the living water of your deepest longings.

 • come and consider •

Come to me—
Bring me
Your dried-up sponge
That once resembled hope.
Come to me,

Living water,
Chuckling, tumbling water.
Let me hydrate your faith,
Plump up your circulation.
Come to me.
I have springs of living water,
Flowing from the rock,
Welling up into life,
Real life,
Eternal life.
Life better than you could ever imagine,
Wet enough to quench the most
Fiery thirst.
Come, play with me
Under the fountain of this living water.
Laugh with me
And splash in this river,
This ever-widening river.
And...please bring your friends.
They are thirsty too.

• come for life •

O God, you are my God, earnestly I seek you; my soul thirsts for you, my body longs for you, in a dry and weary land where there is no water.... Because your love is better than life, my lips will glorify you. I will praise you as long as I live, and in your name I will lift up my hands. My soul will be satisfied as with the richest of foods; with singing lips my mouth will praise you.

Psalm 63:1, 3–5 (NIV)

• come closer •

- When has physical thirst overwhelmed you, dominated your every thought? What about spiritual thirst? What does that feel like to you?
- In what ways do you attempt to assuage your thirst? Habits, compulsions, the hands-on stuff around you? How do you obey your thirst? What are the warning signs in your soul?
- How do you tune in to your real thirst?
- How do you fill that thirst with Christ? What does it look like, feel like?
- When do you offer living water to others? How attractive is that water, given the way you relate to others and the state of your heart and life?

• come home •

Father,
Thank you. Thank you
for the gift of thirst.
For the signs
that my body needs water,
and thank you for the symptoms
that my soul is parched with
longing for you.
Please, Father,
fill my cup with
this living water
that I would thirst
after you,

and that your life
would pour from me
in vital streams of
grace, kindness,
love, compassion,
and generosity.
I come and drink.
Jesus promises rivers of living water flowing,
straight from him, through us, and out into a thirsty
world.
In his name,
my living water,
amen.

• come today •

How will you come today for a drink?

come
for breakfast

"Jesus said to them, 'Come and
have breakfast.' Jesus...took
the bread and gave it to them,
and the fish likewise."
—John 21:12–13

• • • • •

Jesus, dear expected guest,
    Thou art bidden to the feast;
    For Thyself our hearts prepare;
    Come, and sit, and banquet there.
        CHARLES WESLEY

woke up about five hours before my alarm was set to go off. This is
not usually a good sign of the occupations and state of my subcon-
scious mind. At one in the morning, not much else transpires around
our house or neighborhood, and with my husband and son out of
town, only the white-noise whirring of the fan filled the airwaves.

Sighing and flouncing around in bed to face the window, I saw that fog gauzed over the space between earth and sky. No moon shadows, no stars. Just fog. It was like a commercial: "This is your brain. This is your brain on worry."

To be awake so early does not indicate that I am well rested and ready to go, especially since I'd fallen asleep only two hours prior. Rather, my mind has elevated hand-wringing worry to a new level, like an orange alert, and has propelled me into full patrol.

This seems like a good use of my energy.

I know all the axioms, like, "Give your worries to God—he'll be up all night anyway." But as clever and true as this is, I seem to have to work through many sets of worry beads before I hang them up and open my fidgety fingers to him. Worry is like an unrelenting and annoying cat that absolutely will not leave you alone when you are sitting on the floor, but insists on climbing all over you, your floor projects, your face, no matter how many times you push it away, saying, "Dumb kitty. Stop. Leave me alone." You can close the cat in the bathroom, but its mews and pleas and scratching and tumbling crawl on your brain.

No great revelations came in the night; the fog didn't lift internally or externally, and when I finally did roll out of bed at 6 a.m., I still couldn't distinguish the ground from the sky because of the cloud cover.

With my decaf coffee and chocolate chips and Bible, I sat near the picture window and journaled. Neither fog lifted. The journal received my anxiety but didn't much relieve it. I read the Scriptures, but in my preoccupation God didn't seem to highlight any words for my spirit. After an hour with my substances and no lofty revelation from the Lord, I decided to just get to my desk and plunge into the day.

This may not be the best prescription for a new day: wrestling through the night with problems and then eating worry for breakfast.

Another Night, Another Breakfast

Night fishing isn't my idea of nocturnal fun, but maybe it's better than the worry wringer. Seven of the disciples hang out at the Sea of Galilee, and, at some point, Peter says, "I am going fishing" (John 21:3). I can't decide if this is regressive behavior or not: he was a fisherman back in the day, before Jesus called the disciples and told them that if they follow Christ, they'll be catching men.

At any rate, the men jump into the fishing boat and shove off. They hunch in their boat for the entire night, and every time they tug on the nets to check for a catch, the nets offer no resistance. They are empty. What happens in their minds?

The days have crawled by since Christ's crucifixion, with the haunting emptiness of their lives in his absence, and the bad memories of their defection after that awful night when the guards came and arrested Jesus. When they discovered that Jesus had vacated the tomb and risen from the dead, the terrified disciples had locked themselves into a room.

They were a bit surprised to suddenly find Jesus walking through the wall to visit with them there, to reassure them of his life and his presence and the promise of the Holy Spirit to comfort and guide and empower them (see John 20:19–25).

"Peace be with you," Jesus had said.

But tonight's a new night, and maybe night brings nightmares. Do they spend this one wondering about all the events of the past days and even the past three years; about their livelihoods, and their callings, and whether their hopes and former careers have just dried up since they didn't catch any fish? There's nothing quite as discouraging as fishing all night and not catching anything except mosquito bites, I would think. Not even a flippin' flounder.

They might as well have been fishing in the desert. As they yank in their dripping mesh once again, finding nothing, the light begins to turn on along the horizon. Dawn erupts over the water, and a voice calls from the shore, "Children, you do not have any fish, do you?"

"Great," they must mutter to each other. "Now we have to tell whoever it is that we're flops. Fishing is a failure. Maybe we are failures. What are we doing here, anyway?"

Still, they answer in dismal tones, "No."

The man on the beach shouts, "Cast the net on the right-hand side of the boat and you will find a catch."

Without a flounder finder, a depth reader, their dawn visitor can't possibly know this. Maybe something niggles at them—another fishing tale, a water story. But the disciples shrug their aching shoulders and throw the nets out again over the right side of their fishing boat. Stranger things have happened to them over these past years. Besides, what do they have to lose?

So once again they fling their nets into the waters. But this time, when they heave on the ropes like the seven dwarfs, they can't haul the net into the boat because of the tumbling, teeming fish.

Recognition

Even so, these men haven't figured it out—until John squints again at the man on the beach and then nudges Peter. "It is the Lord!"

Peter's reaction is pure spontaneity: he pulls on his tunic and hurls himself into the sea, swimming straight for shore.

The others follow in the boat, dragging their catch behind. The smell of fresh fish sizzling over hot coals drifts across the waters.

And Jesus says, as they wade ashore, "Come and have breakfast" (see John 21:1–14).

What happens inside them when they know the Lord's presence, when they see the fish and the bread and the hot fire, and recognize their Lord and Master standing, tending the grill, watching them with those familiar bright eyes?

What is more welcoming than a hot meal, prepared as a surprise gift, a love offering? That meal says many things to its recipients: you are special; you are as welcome as a Popsicle in August; I love you immensely; I have eagerly anticipated this sustenance with you. That hot meal means even more when the relationship ended on a bad note, a note of abandonment and betrayal.

Because when the going got rough—when Jesus's captors bound him and dragged him to the Jewish authorities the disciples could not bring themselves to walk alongside him. They could not follow him, after all, to the cross, in spite of their brave protests and affirmations in calmer moments, safer places.

Jesus had predicted that none of them would be left, and particularly that Peter would deny him three times before the rooster opened its mouth on that day we call Good Friday.

Morning is just another opportunity for the past to haunt us, for the future to glare at us, for the present to taunt us. We stare in the gaunt face of another waking nightmare. When morning pushes us out of bed, shame and pain dog our steps to the kitchen and through the day. Failure flogs us. We shove it away, this heel-nipping companion, but it returns, eager to trip us, tracking us like an anklet for house arrest. On our bad days, after our no-fish-in-the-net nights, we lug the night with us wherever we go.

Reconciliation

When the disciples row ashore, their new catch drags their boat low in the water. They haul in the haul and see the miracle, count the fish flailing about in the net: 153.

Abundance!

And this, from the One who said, long ago, when they first began to know him, when he first found them, fishermen plying the waters with oars and nets, "Follow Me, and I will make you fishers of men." Hope pours slowly, a sunrise, over the shadows in their soul as these thoughts whisper past them like a sea breeze.

The hot fish and the fresh bread and the offer of both from Jesus's hands must humble the men there in that spanking-new daybreak. As Christ breaks the bread and offers it to the worry-weary men, something must break within each of them.

Their hearts?

Yes, for they cannot grasp that bread without seeing the holes in his hands, remembering the hole in his side, he who said, "This is My body which is given for you" (Luke 22:19). This man sent from God told them that he came to die for them so they could really live—he had promised that he would never quit loving them. They, however, had quit loving him, at least if love is measured by obedience, by presence, by holding fast to truth and trust and calling.

Perhaps, too, their pride finally breaks, and they know that without Jesus, all the fish in the world mean nothing. Without him, dawn means the start of another day's drudgery. Nothing means anything without Christ. These disciples have nothing to offer except a bunch of empty nets.

That's all they really need. All any of us need. Empty nets. We can't offer Jesus anything except our emptiness, with hopes that he will fill those sagging, empty dreams with himself.

And so this day, with the tang of salt air and the roasting fish mingling together, they take the bread from their Master's hand, and eat. And as they eat, the holes in their hearts mend, worn fishing nets carefully stitched by experienced, sea-worn hands. As they receive that offering of food, as they break their fast, they receive, once again, their Christ.

He is back from the dead. And so are they.

Sunrise. The start of a new day, a resurrection: from the sleep of night, the dark of the cross, the ugly pain of rejection and defection, of denial, disbelief, of work and worry that don't work.

With the dawn light on Jesus's face, he invites them, invites me, invites you, invites us, to live in the light of this new day. Dark, worry, sin behind you, shadows cast out by the sun, by the Son.

Come.

Have breakfast.

 • come and consider •

Come, child.
Leave your work
And your worries and climb
Out of the boat and
Into my life.
Sit beside me,
Tell me about your
Nights, and your days,
And your fears and failures.
Tell me your fishing stories,
Your hopes and your dreams,
The big one that got away.

You have been away too long,
And now that it is day,
Let us break our fast

Together.
Leave your empty nets
And let me fill you
Full to the brim
With a life that
Never ends.
Take,
And eat.

• come for life •

Remember my affliction and my wandering, the wormwood and bitterness. Surely my soul remembers and is bowed down within me. This I recall to my mind, therefore I have hope. The LORD's lovingkindnesses indeed never cease, for His compassions never fail. They are new every morning; great is Your faithfulness. 'The LORD is my portion,' says my soul, 'Therefore I have hope in Him.' The LORD is good to those who wait for Him, to the person who seeks Him. It is good that he waits silently for the salvation of the LORD."

Lamentations 3:19–26

• come closer •

- Describe what happens within your soul from your first wake-up call until your day starts in earnest.
- What night do you haul about with you? Regrets, unfinished business? What worries occupy your thoughts? What failure in particular haunts you?
- When do you feel your empty nets? What do you hope Jesus will pour into those nets? How can your empty nets become a gift?

- Someone said, "If you know how to worry, you know how to meditate." Other ways to break fast with Jesus could be silence, reading Scripture, walking and praying.
- Describe a meaningful "breakfast" you've experienced with Christ.

• come home •

Lord Jesus,
I wonder about my own eyes
and all the times I can't see you
on the shore.
You fix me breakfast
but I'm noshing on worry instead,
rushing into work,
diving headlong into water over my head
with no Savior in sight.
Thank you, Lord,
that you are always on the beach
grilling up a mess of fish,
always hoping to feed me breakfast,
lunch, dinner,
to restore me to relationship,
to invite me back to you.
Because night falls on me
throughout the day
and I lose you in the darkness.
But I awaken, today,
to the roasting smell of
fish and bread and
sunlight spilling and smiling over my face

and I come,
and have breakfast at
this picnic
by the sea.

• come today •

How will you come today for breakfast?

PART 4
· · · · ·

homecoming
Heaven

come
home

"I will come again and receive
you to Myself, that where I am,
there you may be also."
—John 14:3

• • • • •

Come, Thou long-expected Jesus
    Born to set Thy people free;
    From our fears and sins release us;
    Let us find our rest in Thee.
    Israel's strength and consolation,
    Hope of all the earth Thou art.
    Dear desire of every nation,
    Joy of every longing heart.
            CHARLES WESLEY

Carl's diagnosis arrived while he was in mock retirement. He and his wife, Sharon, had officially retired, and before they'd had time to wind their new watches, they jumped into their second master's degrees, began volunteering at a homeless shelter, and started learning the craft of pottery. Life was full; life was good. But the doctors' words were grave: Parkinson's disease and cancer.

People cluck-clucked and wrung their hands and "poor Carl-ed" him. Carl shrugged his shoulders and headed off to his night class. He had a master's degree to work toward. When friends decided to travel to Japan, Carl and Sharon signed up in spite of medical issues. No grass would grow under his feet, even if the Parkinson's made him more wobbly, even if the cancer treatment nibbled away at his strength. He could either die sitting down in his chair, slumped over in depression, or he could see Japan and see what God had for him next. If heaven were the next stop, wonderful.

A whirlwind tour of Tokyo introduced them to foreign delicacies they couldn't pronounce, beauty and poverty and new customs. Their hearts filled with all the newness of life overseas. Then Carl woke up one morning and couldn't speak.

They rushed him to a nearby naval hospital, amazingly nearby, in fact. Almost as if part of the plan. Carl hovered near death while the experts consulted and treated him, giving Sharon an unattractive prognosis.

Neither of them regretted the trip to Japan. Carl wanted to die being fully alive.

But he didn't die. He came back to life with proper electrolyte balancing and some other tinkering, though their prolonged stay in Japan meant they had to postpone their fiftieth wedding anniversary celebration. Note: *postpone*, not *cancel.*

Heaven would be nice, he says. Cancer may well be his ticket there. He's not going to fight against death. But, meanwhile, his temporary address is Earth, and right now he has a lot of living left in him. He is living life against the grain. Totally against the culture.

In this culture, death is an aberration, some sort of defect. We fight against death with both fists. And we are lawsuit-happy—happy to sue anyone or any manufacturer who moves us closer to that finality. Everything comes with warnings: the cords on our miniblinds, the air bags on the minivan, the slice-and-dice blades on our mini food processors. Shoot, my mattress came with a warning! Our world obsesses with prolonging our lives and avoiding suffering, no matter the cost.

The great immutable, inescapable truth of life on Earth is dying: we cannot avoid it unless Jesus returns before we kick the bucket. While we spend enormous energy trying to avoid death and prolong life, we may be missing something crucial in God's shorthand communication with us: the body is not designed to live forever, and within each of us is a longing for home.

Jesus's words to his followers offer insight about living in this place and hope about coming home.

Come Again?

The group still clusters in the borrowed room—the upper room as it has come to be called. Jesus, his disciples, and likely a crowd of other followers, such as the women who helped finance the ministry, washed the laundry, and probably made the Passover meal. They have come from much hoopla, when folks lined the streets with palms, cheering as Jesus rode by on an unbroken donkey. Jesus told the multitudes that the Light would be with them only a little while longer. Of course, no one understood.

Now, alone in this crowded space, cram-jammed with a crayon box assortment of people, Jesus tries again. He condenses teaching about forgiveness, about his betrayal, and segues into his imminent departure. "Little children, I am with you a little while longer. You will seek Me; and as I said to the Jews, now I also say to you, 'Where I am going, you cannot come'" (John 13:33). Jesus goes on to tell them the key identifying factor for anyone choosing to follow him: "By this all men will know that you are My disciples, if you have love for one another" (verse 35).

Peter inserts a conversational backward somersault: "Lord, where are You going?" (verse 36) as though this is the first time he's heard anything about it. You have to love him for continuing to ask clarifying questions and love Jesus for not squeezing Peter's face between his palms and squinching his mouth together, asking, "Weren't you listening to a word I said?"

Jesus again says, "Where I go, you cannot follow Me now; but you will follow later."

Peter answers in Peter-fashion, "Lord, why can I not follow You right now? I will lay down my life for You."

Jesus knocks on the door of Peter's arrogance: "Will you lay down your life for Me? Truly, truly, I say to you, a rooster will not crow until you deny Me three times."

Anxiety rises like fevers during a plague, like mercury in the desert (except maybe they hadn't discovered mercury yet).

The Word, the living and breathing Word, speaks to their unspoken but pulsating fear: "Do not let your heart be troubled; believe in God, believe also in Me. In My Father's house are many dwelling places; if it were not so, I would have told you; for I go to prepare a place for you. If I go and prepare a place for you, I will come again and receive you to Myself, that where I am, there you may be also" (John 14:1–3).

"I will come again and receive you to Myself." He will return, claim us, and take us home. And while we await that time, we learn how to come home to him daily, to come home to his heart.

Death by Obsolescence

Good plan, right?

Meanwhile, we save all our lifetime warranties from pillows and can openers and brake jobs, and pretend that the guarantee is good on our bodies. The rest of the world is trying to figure out how to keep from dying, or to sue people who they think somehow hasten them toward eternity. What we forget in our marathon run toward eternal youth rather than eternity, what we overlook as we liposuction and nip and tuck, what we disregard as we evade the advance of years and its ever-present shadow—death—is one salient truth:

While we treat death as an aberration, God sees it as planned obsolescence. The last thing he wants is for us to live forever in these broken and breaking bodies, in this broken and breaking world where nothing works right. And nothing is intended to work right in this place. That's part of the plan.

Cinderella was ticked when her pumpkin came with a limited warranty. So when your fifteen-year-old travel hair-dryer blows itself out, and you have to trudge to the five and dime (oh, wait, that was my childhood) for a replacement, when one of your working parts stops working and you have to jump-start it again, know this: we are designed for planned obsolescence. This was not a marketing invention from the Industrial Revolution or from the Stone Age where people with animal skins wrapped around their loins tried to figure out how to make stone wheels break more easily to ensure repeat sales and job security.

When our bodies malfunction, as messy and mortifying as it may be, to say nothing of countercultural, this is our chance! This is where we get to agree, at last, with God's plan: heaven's coming. And while Jesus is making our beds and prepping our rooms there, he's also getting us ready here on Earth.

Every breakdown, meltdown, shutdown, every struggle or casualty, presents us with the opportunity to move closer to our final goal. Paul tells us, "I press on toward the goal for the prize of the upward call of God in Christ Jesus" (Philippians 3:14). That bifold upward call: to be like Christ *and* to be called finally to our real home.

Planned obsolescence?

Amen, I say. Press on.

Groaning in Our Earthly Tent

In the meantime, we live like turtles, hauling around increasingly heavy shells on our backs: heavy with the bruises of this lifetime, hurting relationships, and some unknown pressure speaking of birth. If we live our lives as though living in a glass-bottom boat where we can see clear to the bottom of our hearts, our true longing rises to the surface. Patch Adams, the doctor who founded the Gesundheit Institute, believes in laughter as a cure for disease. In the movie *Patch Adams* with Robin Williams, Patch seems to know very well this longing for a real home:

> All of life is a coming home. Salesmen, secretaries, coal miners, beekeepers, sword swallowers. All of us. All the restless hearts of the world all trying to find a way home. It's hard to describe what I felt like then. Picture yourself walking for days in a driving snow. You don't even know you're walking in circles. The heaviness of your legs in the drifts. Your shouts disappearing into the wind. How small you can feel and how far away from home you can be.[1]

Yes, a faraway home. In our earthly tents, these temporary tabernacles that house our Lord Jesus, we wait to be clothed with heaven's covering. So we live, then, with constant contractions of life waiting to be born, waiting until the time that, as Paul says, "what is mortal will be swallowed up by life" (2 Corinthians 5:4). There it is again! Life! And again: "as dying yet behold, we live" (2 Corinthians 6:9). We get to carry about in our dying bodies the life of Jesus, the life that will never die. This means that every step we take, every rock we leap, every wall we climb becomes a privilege, and we become a walking display of Christ.

Yes, we are far from home. But then again, home has never left us. Home is where God is, and we must learn to excel at the art of being at home in our own heart and body, seeking God's presence more consistently throughout each day, learning to live—to love—in him. There is plenty of opportunity for love, right where we are, even as we ache for heaven.

Dietrich Bonhoeffer wrote,

I believe that we ought to so love God in our lives, and in all the good things that he sends us, that when the time comes (but not before!) we may go to him with love, trust, and joy. But, to put it plainly, for a man in his wife's arms to be hankering after the other world is, in mild terms, a piece of bad taste, and not God's will. We ought to find and love God in what he actually gives us; if it pleases God to allow us to enjoy some overwhelming earthly happiness, we mustn't try to be more pious than God himself and allow our happiness to be corrupted by presumption and arrogance, and by unbridled religious fantasy which is never satisfied by what God gives. God will see to it that the one who finds him in earthly happiness and thanks him for it does not lack reminder that earthly things are transient, that it is good to attune one's heart to what is eternal, and that sooner or later there will be times when one can say in all sincerity, "I wish I were home." But everything has its time, and the main thing is that we keep step with God, and do not keep pressing on a few steps ahead—nor keep dawdling a step behind.[2]

However, keeping step with God, as Bonhoeffer put it, is hard if you keep running away.

Running Away from Home

Earth-speak doesn't translate the language of longings very cleanly, and those longings can lead us on plenty of lemminglike lunges. If I'm not listening closely, I'll misinterpret that insistent pressure on my heart that waits for birth, that groans for heaven. I'll mistake it for a longing for another person, or some new fiddle-dee-dee tent pegs for my tent, or for just a few bites or handfuls of chocolate truffles (I have a two-ingredient recipe if anyone is interested, this being a typical substitute for my heart groans). I'll decide I need to phone a friend when I really need to snuggle in with God.

I will, in effect, run away from home.

Once I stayed at a camp for back-to-back weekend retreats. At the first retreat, God did a "real number on women's hearts," as their pastor put it later. When the camp director gave me that feedback at a community meal midweek, I wanted to bawl from sheer gratitude.

I walked back to my cabin, brimful, deeply humbled by the work that transpired and that God used this earthly container to help communicate with others. As I felt my way through the dark, my only thought was, *I need to call Rich. I have to share these miracles with him. I love him so much,* I thought. *I really want to be with Rich. I miss him while I sleep alone on my little plank bed.*

And on and on I thought, walking through the woods.

Now all of those are true and good. But at my cabin, thick birch trees blocked the cell phone signal, and I snapped my phone closed with a sigh. Then the Holy Spirit pulled my heart into his hands and asked me to come home.

I cried then, because I had misinterpreted my longing—without a hitch I had turned it into a longing for my husband. I wrote in my journal:

> Oh Lord, thank you. I really want to share this joy with you. I wish I could feel your arm about my shoulder, feel your chest solid against my cheek, hear your delight and pride and joy— hear your 'Well done, Janey,' your joy over redeeming the ugliness of my past and your absolute bursting over the women's movement toward you, and the ramifications of this on the lives of their families, friends, coworkers, future. Thank you for holding on to me when I wasn't changing and was having such a negative impact on my own family. Thank you for pain that forced the issue: who am I? And more important, who are you, and who am I when you are in control?

This is good news, though. God got my attention. The more we listen and redirect, not only will we weigh less (fewer truffles) and have less debt (fewer tent peg purchases), but the more we will hear God's howl of laughter and see his dance of delight when we turn to him, run to him, and come home again.

Living It Up

Oh, to stop running and start living, really living, here on Earth while we are separated from our forever home. Jesus reminds us how to do this. Remember Peter's bold assertion, "I will lay down my life for You," and Christ's response, "A rooster will not crow until you deny Me three times" (John 13:37–38)?

Imagine how this devastated Peter and what a damper this put on their dinner party. But hear Christ's next words:

> Do not let your heart be troubled; believe in God, believe also in Me....
>> Peace I leave with you; My peace I give to you;
>> not as the world gives do I give to you.
>> Do not let your heart be troubled, nor let it be fearful.
> (John 14:1, 27)

Did you get it? Regardless of how far away Peter ran, Jesus's words offer the remedy. "Believe in God, believe also in Me." Out of that belief comes peace. Not the kind of peace the world offers: peace from painkillers, peace through your debit card, or peace through the right or different relationship. No, this is a peace far different. Peace in the Scriptures, according to the Hebrews' use of the word, meant everything you need to live well right now.

But that's not possible, is it? There are no marriage offers in queue, or your marriage isn't what you wanted or hoped for, or your boyfriend needs a complete makeover, or your job is the equivalent of the chain gang, or you're one month away from living on the street because of your finances, or there are a few itty-bitty parent-child issues, or...

Jesus says *shalom* to this. *Peace.* Direct that fear to God, direct that longing to God. Look again at him. Faith is to believe that God is who he says he is and will do what he says he will do. And he says, "I am giving you peace. I am speaking peace over you. Will you live in that peace, look to me when you snatch up the worry beads and start to work them?"

Jonathan Edwards, an eighteenth-century New England revivalist and preacher, summarized this prescription for peace in his first sermon at age eighteen: "God will give you everything you would have asked for if you knew everything God knows."

In a world of planned obsolescence, while waiting for our hearts to stop pumping and our synapses to shout "cease fire," what does abundant life look like?

It looks like peace. While we wait for him to come again and take us home, that's a pretty good prize.

• come and consider •

To My Best Girl,
Hoo-ha! I cannot wait to see you face to face.
You are beautiful to me,
And every moment on this earth
Prepares you more to be with me forever
In person.
You are the light of my life
And the reason I came to the earth
In the first place:
So I could bring you home with me,
And we could live there forever.
What a day that will be,
A day that will last for all eternity.

In the meantime,
I had to run ahead of you

To make everything ready.
But I will come back for you—
Don't doubt it for even a moment.
Keep watching for me,
Keep loving those around you,
Keep checking in the mirror
To see if you look more and more
Like me.
And I will see you
Soon.
Until then,
Hold tight.
We have quite an adventure
Ahead of us.
Let's live it up,
Live it fully,
And laugh all the way
Home.

• come for life •

And if the Spirit of him who raised Jesus from the dead is living in you, he who raised Christ from the dead will also give life to your mortal bodies through his Spirit, who lives in you.

Romans 8:11 (NIV)

• come closer •

- Peter missed one of the gifts of staying put here on earth: "if you have love for one another." When you look at your life, how do you display this characteristic?

- Where do you see death by obsolescence operating in your life? How can those events and issues help you become more like Jesus, and what would that look like, anyway?
- When do you notice your true longing for heaven? How do you run away from that longing?
- List some of your moanings and groanings from this week. Now reexamine those issues that you found moanable and groanable: how do they show your longing for home?
- Put down on paper some of the high-fever anxiety you're carrying around with you. Now read Jesus's words again in John 14:1, 27. How is Jesus redirecting your heart toward home in light of your worries and in light of his Word?

· come home ·

Lord Jesus, oh, Lord Jesus—
I have missed it.
I have tried to avoid, evade, escape death;
I have tried to charge others with
wrongful death toward me,
all the while
craving more:
more excitement,
more adventure,
more bang for the buck,
more money to live on,
and more debt to die with,
more toys to assuage my emptiness
and divert my attention.
But those longings are from you,
and I have not listened deeply enough.

Please forgive me, change me.
Help me to live well in this earthly
but dying body,
to seize every opportunity
to showcase, not the latest fashion,
but Jesus
showing through my skin.
Come home to me, Lord.
Swallow up what is mortal,
what is dying,
with life.
Live wholly in me,
Lord Jesus,
that I might move from holey
to whole and holy.
You alone
make this possible.
Thank you.
Amen.

• come today •

How will you come home today?

come,
Lord Jesus

"And behold, I am coming quickly."
—Revelation 22:12

• • • • •

Mine eyes have seen the glory
    Of the coming of the Lord…
    He is coming like the glory of the
    Morning on the wave,
    He is wisdom to the mighty,
    He is honor to the brave;
    So the world shall be his footstool,
    And the soul of wrong his slave.
    Our God is marching on.
        JULIA WARD HOWE

My grandparents' farm in Franklin County, Tennessee, lolled over hundreds of acres. On many a vacation, my brother and sister and I tumbled over as many of those acres as possible, loving the freedom, the greenery, the barn and the pigs and the jersey cow, the henhouse and warm beige eggs. We would wrench open the smoke-house door and breathe the salt-cured scents of smoked ham. Some-times, in the summer, one of us spent a week there. On one of my trips, entranced, I watched the milking process as the steady stream pinged into the bucket. Shoulders tense, trying not to slosh, I helped carry the warm milk to the dark cooling room off the kitchen. In the back, rickety stairs descended into the dirt-floor cellar, and the room smelled of wood and dust motes and mysteries, organic and ancient as the ground below.

Wide planks creaked under our steps, and I trailed Mom-Mom (our name for our grandmother) through her daily chores. Straining the milk, then watching the cream rise in the pail. Helping skim off the cream to pour later over fresh berries. Churning butter. Helping make biscuits in the green bowl—the best biscuits in the entire world, steaming bites of heaven with butter dribbling from the pillowy insides.

While we worked inside, the temperature climbed outside, and the harder we worked, the hotter we got. While Mom-Mom stood over the bathtub-deep kitchen sink, sweat poured from her brow and filled in the wrinkles on her face. Keeping her hands free and clean, she raised her forearm and mopped the sweat that rolled over the tip of her nose.

"Phew."

That was all. No complaints, just a sigh as big as a lion's. From the heat? the endless labor? a longing for respite, a different life, another world?

I don't know. I was young and skinny with bad posture and an emaciated question pool, but the volumes contained in that single long exhale still speak to me.

"Phew."

Sometimes I awaken to the sense that before me hangs an invisible veil, and beyond its gossamer draping lies another world: vast, measureless, with brilliance that would blind us. It's as though I stand at the edge of an opening in the wall of time, toes gripping the rim of a ledge. Behind me, the familiar world. Before me, a canyon unlike anything our eyes could stand to behold because its beauty would slay us.

In my head I hear the words, "And Lord, haste the day, when my faith shall be sight," from the hymn, "It Is Well with My Soul." And even though Jesus said he was coming quickly, it sure is taking a long time by human years.

And I want to wipe my brow with my raised forearm, and let out a sigh as big as a lion, "Phew! I can't wait for heaven."

Could It Be that Jesus Comes Now?

Jesus said he is coming quickly; yet, while we wait, the kingdom of heaven is all around us: in the face of a jonquil, the gurgles of a baby, in the hummingbird dipping in and out of the trumpet vine, in the man without teeth outside the grocery store, hoping for loose change to jingle in his cup.

The kingdom of God appears in the many small kindnesses exchanged throughout a day: The sister who buys a sack of fun foods and surprises her brother when he opens his lunch box. The phone call from a friend: "I was praying for you this morning." A soft touch on someone's shoulder as we pass by. Side-clutching laughter with your best friend. Making love with your husband.

When we meet the eyes of a stranger on the street corner and smile, the kingdom comes. Just a smile, and we hasten the kingdom.

We make this coming sound so theoretical, so complicated, so far away—and there is much to the theology, the eschatology, of course—and yet daily Jesus waits, wanting to break into our world, to rush through that veil and meet us here, on this turf, to smile into our eyes with his own brightness until the day he takes us to his own realm. If our eyes were truly open, we would need sunglasses to sleep at night.

After detailing a painful and long passage in her life, one woman described her unending sense of God's guidance in those times: "You have to be wakeful, to be aware of the door ajar rather than the end of the line."

That wakefulness comes when we focus on Christ.

Training Your Eye

Throughout Jesus's tenure here, he never once broke eye contact with God. The eyes of his heart constantly focused on his Father, even as people jostled him in crowds, criticized him for his words or his touch, or for the way he thought or acted. Even as he healed and preached, overturned tables and wept with Mary and Martha. Always he kept a bead on heaven, his hearing heightened for God's direction.

This seamless connection, the discipline of training his spiritual attention on the unseen Father, unsettles and convicts me. I want to live more like this. That seamlessness means that I cannot tell where I end and Jesus begins; I cannot discern where we are stitched together, the old rag that is my soul and the new cloth that is Jesus.

Often my life is a crazy quilt of hodgepodge fabrics, most of them tacky, and when I am stitched to Jesus, suddenly those fabrics are transformed to lovely silk. When I am training my eye on Jesus, instead of being clumsy in speech with someone, or wordless when words are called for, Christ comes into my words.

On an airplane last week, the woman in the aisle seat leaned across the poor man trying to sleep in between us, and poured out some pain in a relationship. If I'd stopped to consider that I am twenty years younger than she is or that she works for a prestigious organization—in other words, stopped to look at myself—I'd have drawn a blank. But instead, I paid attention to her heart and to Christ, and I said the words that showed up. Her face responded like the sun rising into a dark sky.

The closer we tune in to our inner workings, the more present we are to why we do and say the things we say, the more we allow ourselves to move into a still, silent place in our soul, the more seamless the transfer from us to Jesus.

In the Scripture we read, "Keep seeking the things above, where Christ is, seated at the right hand of God. Set your mind on the things above, not on the things that are on earth" (Colossians 3:1–2).

Gym class was the bane of my existence. I was uncoordinated, awkward, and way behind in physical development. No one wanted me on the team, and this was totally understandable. I could run fairly fast but not very far, and that was the extent of my talent. In college, guys noticed my height and tailed me from the cafeteria to wheedle me into playing basketball on the women's team. I laughed. "Believe me, you do not want me on your team."

I never got the gist of any sports containing flying objects, like softballs, basketballs, tennis balls: keep your eye on the ball.

If you keep your eye on the ball, then with the tiniest bit of hand-eye coordination, your hand will respond to what your eye sees and reach out and grab, or hit, the ball.

Living Toward Heaven

Living toward heaven now is not unlike that principle. We keep our eyes on Jesus. We seek always to meet his eyes, pulling our attention back to his face, like Brother Lawrence in *The Practice of the Presence of God.*

Maybe this looks like an ongoing conversation in your heart and head where you discuss your current situation, move into prayer as you notice people in the next car arguing, praise God for the sunset over the sunflower field, repeat the words of Scripture that you are committing to memory, confess an unkind thought, or repent quickly of an interchange with someone. It is hard to look another straight in the eyes if there is sin between you, and by living toward heaven, we become more honest with both Jesus and with others.

When we keep our eyes focused on Jesus, something happens with the eyes of our soul. Something happens as we gaze, then, at others around us. A transformation that begins in us spills over onto them, like light from a ballroom suddenly pours into the hallway when the door is opened. Seeing Jesus corrects our eyesight, and we see others not as people who inconvenience us or need us or remind us of the work of relationships—I have to feed you, or sew the button on your shirt, or help you with your science project, or correct something about you, or the millions of responsibilities that go with being human among humans—we see them, instead, with Jesus's eyes.

When we focus on heaven—Thy kingdom come—earthly things assume proper dimension. Thomas á Kempis said,

> Father, you may give me many things in my life—things I desire, things that surprise and delight me. But whatever you give me besides yourself will be small in comparison. Your gifts will make my heart glad for a time, but that happiness will fade. It will not be enough to give me the life from within, which I need to sustain me through the battle of this life…to keep me strong on this long journey. What is it I need? Above all created things, my heart needs to find its home…in you.… You alone are my victory in every battle.… You are my journey's end.[1]

If Christ is our journey's end, then every time our life breaks, every time we face disappointment in relationships, every time we ache over the past or fear for the future, we turn to God in prayer. There, we know that our home, our help, our comfort come from him. "God, help me, hold me, let me know your love right now," we might beg. When we find our home in Christ, and our lives are in shambles, we find perspective in the truth that God is still in control.

The psalmist finds his home in God in Psalm 25:16–18, 20, which says, "Turn to me and be gracious to me, for I am lonely and afflicted. The troubles of my heart have multiplied; free me from my anguish. Look upon my affliction and my distress and take away all my sins.... Guard my life and rescue me; let me not be put to shame, for I take refuge in you" (NIV).

This is a bit like cuddling up in front of a fireplace knowing that the fireplace is God, and it is Christ who cuddles us. There we are warmed and filled and recharged, and then head off to work—to meet others' eyes, see their need, and love them.

"When he saw the crowds, he had compassion on them" (Matthew 9:36, NIV). Literally, suffered with. "Jesus looked at him and loved him" (Mark 10:21, NIV). Love like this changes the world. Loving like this brings Christ. Life like this, focused on him, on heaven, is not pie-in-the-sky thinking. It's not, as C. S. Lewis said,

> ...a form of escapism or wishful thinking. It does not mean
> that we are to leave the present world as it is. If you read his-
> tory...the Christians who did most for the present world were
> just those who thought most of the next. The Apostles them-
> selves, who set on foot the conversion of the Roman Empire,
> the great men who built up the Middle Ages, the English
> Evangelicals who abolished the Slave Trade, all left their mark
> on Earth, precisely because their minds were occupied with

Heaven. It is since Christians have largely ceased to think of the other world that they have become so ineffective in this.[2]

The Pharisees tried to pinpoint when the kingdom might come. Jesus answered, "The kingdom of God is in your midst" (see Luke 17:20–21). In us, through us, all around us.

A New Heaven and a New Earth

The Lord spoke to John and gave him new eyes—eyes to expect the Lord's return:

> Then I saw a new heaven and a new earth; for the first heaven and the first earth passed away, and there is no longer any sea. And I saw the holy city, new Jerusalem, coming down out of heaven from God, made ready as a bride adorned for her husband. And I heard a loud voice from the throne, saying, "Behold, the tabernacle of God is among men, and He will dwell among them, and they shall be His people, and God Himself will be among them, and He will wipe away every tear from their eyes; and there will no longer be any death; there will no longer be any mourning, or crying, or pain; the first things have passed away." And He who sits on the throne said, "Behold, I am making all things new." (Revelation 21:1–5)

The One who is making all things new begins that creative process every second of every day. And don't the Scriptures say, "This means that anyone who belongs to Christ has become a new person. The old life is gone; a new life has begun!" (2 Corinthians 5:17, NLT)? A new creation, just like a new heaven, a new earth—when we live a clean life, a life where we reach out to love, to ease someone's pain, to lift someone's burden, heaven comes in a puff of air. Phew.

While we live in this weeping, mourning, pain-filled and painful world, every time we weep with another who weeps, does God not make all things new? Every time we repent of causing pain, Christ comes near. Every tear we dry, every laugh we share, every time we live out the truth of Christ, the greatest miracle in the universe—Jesus loves you!—he comes. He comes and lives among us.

When we wipe the sweat from our brow as we toil over the work God has given us to do, when we whistle in the midst of it, when we sing and make music in our hearts toward God, when we choose to end a fight by relinquishing the need to be right, when we dance even though we dance badly, when we forgive, the spring green of newness comes, the brightness of heaven. Grab your sunglasses.

Every time our words bring life instead of death, Christ comes. Each time we believe the best of someone, Christ comes. Every time we rejoice with someone over God's goodness in her life, Christ comes. Bring your sunscreen.

Little things comprise our lives, and little things draw the kingdom closer. Matthew Henry, an English clergyman from the 1600s, said, "It is certain that all that will go to heaven hereafter begin their heaven now."

The more we live in this out-of-order world with our eyes fixed on Jesus, the more we will live in heaven now, though our feet remain on earthly soil. The more tears we wipe, the more sorrow we share, the more death we alleviate, then the deeper our longing to live forever in the skin-on presence of the Lord. No more tears, no more sorrow, no more death.

Cloud of Witnesses

Once when I entered an ancient church on the coast of Georgia, a hush descended over my body and soul. I was not alone there, though no one occupied a single bench. Dust glittered in the faint light from the stained glass windows, an ethereal cloud. I blinked, took kitten-soft steps to a darkened pew. As I settled myself, breathing in the cool, moist air, whispering "Come, Lord Jesus," eternity opened for me, a split in the wall of time.

The invisible great cloud of witnesses crowded about me, peopling this chapel, inviting me into a holy space. Even now, I feel that pressure, that internal knowing that says, "Yes."

> Therefore, since we have so great a cloud of witnesses sur-
> rounding us, let us also lay aside every encumbrance and the
> sin which so easily entangles us, and let us run with endurance
> the race that is set before us, fixing our eyes on Jesus, the
> author and perfecter of faith, who for the joy set before Him
> endured the cross, despising the shame, and has sat down at
> the right hand of the throne of God. (Hebrews 12:1–2)

While we run this race with our focus on Jesus, we do not run alone, nor do we run with only the hope of heaven someday, off in the future, when the roll is called up yonder. No, heaven comes today when you drop off your extra baggage, untangle yourself from sin, when you "take hold of the eternal life to which you were called, and you made the good confession in the presence of many witnesses" (1 Timothy 6:12). We seize that life, bringing heaven here, accessing the fullness of abundant life, kingdom life, eternity, though our race is far from over.

Barricades barred the road. A few leftover competitors straggled toward the finish line, the rest crossing minutes and even hours ago. A woman and a boy plodded past. He was thin, maybe eight years old—an earnest eight and desperate to run well. The mom clearly could have run faster, but her pace matched the boy's stride.

Behind them, other runners, who bobbled and jiggled more than jogged by this time, cheered, "Go, Timmy! Go, Timmy!" The boy's face contorted in effort, blotchy from exertion. Sweat streamed down.

"Go, Timmy! You're almost there!" Some runners had completed their race and doubled back to the sidelines to help bring the last ones down victory lane. The finish line waited one block away, clearly visible, but Timmy's energy sputtered. He wound down to a walk.

The cheering section hollered encouragement: "You can do it!"

Timmy hesitated. His mom waited, nearly walking in place. Her lips moved, soft words to sink into him and draw forth his best. Perhaps she knew the demoralizing effect of quitting too soon, too close to the finish.

As I watched from behind, his back straightened with determination, snapping to attention as though to an officer's command. His legs started to churn again, thudding, left, right, left, right, a final spurt of guts for the glory of that ending.

I stood, briefcase on the sidewalk next to me, still waiting to cross the street, while he ran the entire block. I cheered him over the finish line. Tears tightened my throat. The long week of my cheering other "runners" at a conference had concluded that evening, and I felt the fatigue of the race in the legs of my soul, the beat of my heart.

Who doesn't long to be cheered? The teamwork of the mom, who slowed her pace, loving her son at whatever pace he ran, encouraging and supporting him from the side, speaks powerfully. I can't picture her now, however—just the wiry little boy, so like my own boys; so like all of us, really. Just trying to pump our legs and keep thumping on the path to the finish, to cross that line the final time.

And the other runners, bigger, stronger, faster, following behind, the shouting and cheering from the side, "You can do it!" The guardian at your elbow, clearly able to run faster and leave you in the dust that last block, indeed the whole race, but instead matching your stride, encouraging you forward.

"You can do it!" they yell. "Keep going! You're almost there!"

And as the great crowd of witnesses cheers, a final burst of gusto and glory kicks in. You lunge for the finish line with a lion-sized "phew."

Even so, come, Lord Jesus.

• come and consider •

How I love you, Child.
How I love you.
I am by your side constantly,
Your faithful guide.
Keep running
the race before you—
Keep making a difference,
Day in, day out.
If you listen to your heart,
If you listen with the ears of your soul,
You will hear my heart beating
Strongly,
Cheering you forward,
Strengthening you for
The final kick across
The finish.

Meanwhile, the way is long
And the road winding.
But don't quit.

Don't forget to invite
Me to help you run,
To strengthen you,
To cheer you on.
Keep meeting my eyes,
And you'll have all you
Need for the race.

And listen:
Do you hear
Them?
The cloud of witnesses?
They, too, surround
You with support and
Cheer you on,
Though you can't always
See them.
Hold fast,
Run well,
And grab my hand.
I'm not telling
When the trumpet will sound,
But until then,
We have lots to do.
Let's get loving.

• come for life •

Our Father which art in heaven, Hallowed be thy name. Thy kingdom come. Thy will be done in earth, as it is in heaven. Give us this day our daily bread. And forgive us our debts, as we forgive our debtors. And lead us not into temptation, but deliver us from evil: For thine is the kingdom, and the power, and the glory, for ever. Amen.

Matthew 6:9–13 (KJV)

• come closer •

- When do you long for heaven? What do you do with your heart?
- Where do you see a focus on heaven making earth a better place? How might it change the way you live, the way you love, the way you serve others?
- Who wipes away tears from your eyes, rejoices and weeps with you? When do you sense that your actions bring Christ closer?
- How do the gifts God gives distract you from the treasure of Christ himself? When are you aware that Jesus is your "journey's end," as á Kempis said, or when he isn't?
- What encumbers your race? What sin entangles? How do you throw it off? Who are your visible "cloud of witnesses" cheering you to a good finish?

• come home •

Phew!
Lord, I am wiping my brow
and searching the sky
and wondering,
"How much longer?"
But when I lift my gaze,
I meet your eyes:

smiling at me,
loving me,
full of joy over
my wobbly
gait.
Teach me when to rest,
when to stop along the way,
when to redirect my steps
while I wait.
I long to see your face,
but…I think I see your face
every time I look into someone
else's eyes,
every time I love,
every time I offer healing.
It is only in you
that I have the abundance I crave.
Let me not pine for the things you give;
may my deepest longing
always be, only,
for you,
your presence,
your smile,
your "Well done."
Even so.
Come, Lord Jesus.

• come today •

How will you, today, invite Jesus to come soon?

The Girlfriends' Guide to
Come Closer

How to use this book in group discussion

C *ome Closer* is designed as a personal reading experience and growth tool—and also with the thought and hope of community. Christ did not travel alone when he came to earth; he gathered people around him, and they walked together, talking of life experiences and God's kingdom in their midst. So whether your group forms through a book club, or women at the bus stop, or friends who frequent the neighborhood coffee shop, or as part of a small group structure through a church or women's ministry program, you'll find a rich menu here for personal nourishment and growth in community.

This section will help you dig in. Pick and choose as fits the makeup and personality and needs of your group. You can divide reading and discussion of this book into either an eight- or fifteen-week group commitment to experience life, love, and breakfast on the beach together.

gathering

As you gather, open with prayer, and then read the words of Christ that open each chapter. Depending on the size of the group, consider forming a circle and having each person say aloud Christ's "come" invitation as the words pass around the circle.

Then read the hymn aloud or sing the lyrics if you know the tune. Otherwise, you might divide the group in half and reading them line by line to each other as a type of call and response liturgy.

group discussion

Discussion can proceed informally. Whether you have an official leader or someone facilitates from the side, the elements in the book lend themselves to group process. There's nothing better than girlfriends catching up, and you can catch up through the text in the book. Ask one another:

- What spoke to you?
- What did you underline?
- Where do you have questions?
- Where did God stir your heart, move you to tears?

application

Experiment with different formats as you move through the text and into the closing sections. Don't feel bound by the suggestions here. Not everyone feels comfortable praying aloud or sharing before an entire group. Try these ways to help everyone focus on the message, not the perceptions of the group, and get the most possible out of the material:

come and consider—Turn to one another by twos. Have one person read the section to the other, then reverse. Let this be a time of blessing, a verbalization of a conversation with Jesus. Then turn back to the group for the next section.

come for life—Read this selection aloud as a group. Try it standing up, as Christians in Israel do whenever the Scripture is read. Or have one person read this section aloud while the rest of the group sits with their eyes closed, listening. Then wait for the Word to begin to dwell within you. Listen for a longing to arise, a specific word or phrase to speak to you, stir you. Share that word with your neighbor. Repeat the process a couple of times, and then silently ask God, *How do you want to apply this to my life?* Pray for one other specifically in relation to the scripture and the application.

come closer—Ask these questions of the group, and be willing to wait patiently for the answers to come. Silence is not a bad element during this time, so don't rush to fill it with words. God may be dealing with women's hearts, and they need to be still. You may be tempted to try to fix the problems that members share, but this probably is not the place for advice, as that tends to turn the focus from the person wrestling with the question, to the person wanting to problem solve. One gift of community is to be still with another, loving and accepting, and receiving struggle and pain without judgment.

come home—Invite the participants to pray this prayer either silently or out loud as a group.

come today—Here's the bottom line. The question in this section gets to one big important thing: what are you going to do with what Christ has revealed to you?

closing

As your time together ends, pray for one another about the application of Jesus's words.

Notes

Chapter 1: Come for Abundance
The epigraph to this chapter is drawn from "Lord, I'm Coming Home" by William Kirkpatrick, public domain hymn (1892).

Chapter 2: Come from Death
The epigraph to this chapter is drawn from "Come, My Way, My Truth, My Life" by George Herbert, public domain hymn (1633).

Chapter 3: Come, Follow Me
The epigraph to this chapter is drawn from "Love Divine, All Loves Excelling" by Charles Wesley, public domain hymn (1747).

Chapter 4: Come and See
The epigraph to this chapter is drawn from "Softly and Tenderly Jesus Is Calling" by Will L. Thompson, public domain hymn (1880).

Chapter 5: Come for Healing
The epigraph to this chapter is drawn from "Who Is He in Yonder Stall" version 2 by Benjamin Hanby, public domain hymn (1866).

 1. The International Bible Commentary cites the differences between Luke's accounting of the centurion's visit to Jesus (7:1–10) and Matthew's (8:5–13). "There seems to be no reason for trying to harmonize the two accounts. In dealing with the centurion's representatives Jesus was dealing with him. For mainly Gentile readers Luke stresses the winning of Jews by a

Gentile's love; for mainly Jewish readers Matthew stresses the acceptance of faith wherever found." The International Bible Commentary with the New International Version, General Editor: F. F. Bruce. Originally edited by F. F. Bruce, H. L. Ellison, G. C. D. Howley. First published 1979. This edition published by Guideposts, Carmel, N.Y.

Chapter 6: Come for Relief

The epigraph to this chapter is drawn from "Come Unto Me, Ye Weary" by Fanny Crosby, public domain hymn (1881).

Chapter 7: Come When You're Lost

The epigraph to this chapter is drawn from "Come Down, O Love Divine" by Bianco of Siena, public domain hymn (fifteenth century).

1. Flora Slosson Wuellner, *Heart of Healing, Heart of Light: Encountering God Who Shares and Heals Our Pain* (Nashville: Upper Room, 1993), quoted in Rueben P. Job, *A Guide to Retreat for All God's Shepherds* (Nashville: Abingdon, 1994), 33.
2. M. Robert Mulholland Jr., *The Deeper Journey: The Spirituality of Discovering Your True Self* (Downers Grove, IL: InterVarsity, 2006), 27.

Chapter 8: Come for Adoption

The epigraph to this chapter is drawn from "Come Thou Almighty King," public domain hymn.

1. See John 13:1–3.

Chapter 9: Come for Help

The epigraph to this chapter is drawn from "Come Holy Spirit, Heavenly Dove" by Isaac Watts, public domain hymn (1707).

1. Karolina Wilhelmina Sandell-Berg, "Day by Day, and with Each Passing Moment," public domain hymn (1865).

2. Thomas á Kempis, *The Imitation of Christ*, quoted in David Hazard, ed., *Come, Lord Jesus* (Minneapolis: Bethany, 1999), 114.

3. Jane Rubietta, "But I Can't Do All Things: The Pain of Inability," *indeed*, September/October 2006, 9. Portions of this article are included in the text.

Chapter 10: Come for Acceptance

The epigraph to this chapter is drawn from "I Need Thee Every Hour" by Annie S. Hawks, public domain hymn (1872).

Chapter 11: Come for Light

The epigraph to this chapter is drawn from "Come Unto Me When Shadows Darkly Gather" by Catherine H. Esling, public domain hymn (nineteenth century).

1. Lois Evans and Jane Rubietta, *Stones of Remembrance: A Rock-Hard Faith from Rock-Hard Places* (Chicago: Moody, 2006), 25.

2. Calvin Miller, *The Unchained Soul: A Devotional Walk on the Journey into Christlikeness From the Great Christian Classics* (Minneapolis: Bethany 1995, 1998), xiv.

Chapter 12: Come for a Drink

The epigraph to this chapter is drawn from "Come Thou Fount of Every Blessing" by Robert Robinson, public domain hymn (1758).

1. Aron Ralston, *Between a Rock and a Hard Place* (New York: Atria Books, 2004), 194.

2. Ralston, *Between a Rock and a Hard Place*, 230.

3. Read Psalm 118:15–29 to get a picture of Christ's amazing timing and his fulfillment of the prayer plea!

4. Ralston, *Between a Rock and a Hard Place,* 193.

Chapter 13: Come for Breakfast

The epigraph to this chapter is drawn from "Come, and Let Us Sweetly Join" by Charles Wesley, public domain hymn (1740).

Chapter 14: Come Home

The epigraph to this chapter is drawn from "Come Thou Long-Expected Jesus" by Charles Wesley, public domain hymn (1744).

1. *Patch Adams,* DVD, directed by Tom Shadyac (1998; Calif.: Universal Studios, 2002).

2. *The Wisdom and Witness of Dietrich Bonhoeffer,* ed. Wayne Whitson Floyd (Minneapolis: Augsburg Fortress, 2000), 36.

Chapter 15: Come, Lord Jesus

The epigraph to this chapter is drawn from "The Battle Hymn of the Republic" by Julia Ward Howe (1861).

1. Thomas á Kempis, *The Imitation of Christ,* quoted in David Hazard, ed., *Come, Lord Jesus* (Minneapolis: Bethany, 1999), 172–73.

2. C. S. Lewis, *Mere Christianity,* First Touchstone Edition (New York: Simon & Schuster, 1996), 119.

About the Author

Known for vulnerability, spiritual depth, and humor, Jane Rubietta is a popular and riveting keynote speaker across the country and internationally. She is also the author of ten books, including *Resting Place, Grace Points,* and *Quiet Places.*

She and her husband, Rich, founded a nonprofit, Abounding Ministries, with the mission of offering people life-changing experiences of God's love in Jesus Christ through music, writing, speaking, and retreats for communities, schools, and churches.

After obtaining her BS degree from Indiana University School of Business, Jane completed postgraduate studies in Germany while also directing an international drama team, taking the gospel into then-Communist countries. She worked on her master's degree at Trinity Evangelical Divinity School in Deerfield, Illinois.

Between writing and speaking engagements, Jane serves as assistant coordinator and faculty of Write-to-Publish Writer's Conference, where she finds enormous joy in helping others follow their God-given dreams. She belongs to Advanced Writers and Speakers Association (AWSA) and Speak Up Speaker Services.

Jane and Rich live in Illinois and are the parents of three children.

Visit Jane online at www.JaneRubietta.com or www.abounding.org, or contact her at:

Abounding Ministries
225 Bluff Ave.
Grayslake, IL 60030
(847) 223-4790
jane@janerubietta.com

If your church, women's ministry, or special events coordinator wants to invite Jane for a conference, retreat, banquet, or training event, contact Speak Up Speaker Services, toll-free at (888) 870-7719; e-mail Speakupinc@aol.com; or visit www.SpeakUpSpeakerServices .com.

Also by Jane Rubietta

Grace Points
Quiet Places
Resting Place
How to Keep the Pastor You Love
Fabulous After 50
Sensational After 60
Between Two Gardens
Stones of Remembrance with Lois Evans